OVERCOME EMOTIONAL EATING

Coach Yourself to Manage Cravings, Eat Mindfully, and Foster a Healthy Relationship with Food

Ж

LIISA KYLE, PH.D.

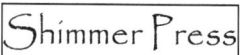

ЖК

Copyright © Liisa Kyle, Ph.D., 2023

ЖК

All rights reserved.
No part of this product may be reproduced, scanned, or distributed in any printed or electronic form without permission.

Thank you for respecting the professional work and intellectual property of this author. If you know someone who would benefit from this book, be kind:
either recommend it to them or buy them their own copy.

ISBN: 9778371027320

ЖК

This book is licensed solely for your personal enjoyment and private self-reflection. This material is not intended as psychological counseling or as a professional coaching relationship with Liisa Kyle, Ph.D. If you require clinical help, please contact a qualified professional immediately. This material is not intended to provide medical advice.

ЖК

BONUS:

If you would like to receive *free* weekly self-quiz questions and self-coaching prompts via email, please sign up here:

http://bit.ly/weeklyprompts

Your information will be kept private. It will not be shared with anyone.

Contents

Chapter 1 - Your Current Relationship with Food......................1

Chapter 2 - Manage Cravings....................................... 15

Chapter 3 - Eat Mindfully.. 31

Chapter 4 - Your Past Relationship with Food....................... 43

Chapter 5 - Your Preferred Relationship with Food................55

Chapter 6 - Implement Your Plans................................... 59

Chapter 7 - Treat Yourself Well......................................73

Chapter 8 - Prepare for Change............................... 95

Chapter 9 - Overcome Setbacks................................. 105

About the Author..115

Chapter 1

What is Your Current Relationship with Food?

Food is essential. We can't live without it. Our connection with food is significant and omnipresent. We interact with food every day of our lives. And, like any relationship that is such a major part of our daily lives, it can be complicated.

Sure, we need food to survive, physically. But food provides so much more than just biological fuel. It plays many other roles that can vary widely among people, across cultures, and at different ages. Eating is enmeshed with varying emotions, thoughts, and beliefs.

Food is a part of most socializing. We often use food to celebrate events, milestones, and accomplishments. Eating together cements social bonds among friends and family. (Ever notice that the people you eat with, say at school or work, tend to become your closest friends or colleagues?)

We might use food to show love to people we care about (*Honey, I made your favorite breakfast*) — or as a way of competing for attention or praise. (*Look! I brought this homemade twelve-layer cake to the potluck!*)

We often use food as a reward (*Yay! I cleaned the bathroom. I've earned some chips*) — and sometimes as a punishment (*I didn't work out today, so I haven't earned dessert*) or worse (*I blew my diet with that cookie at lunch so I might as well go hog wild for the rest of the day, then start over tomorrow.*)

For some, food provides opportunities for creativity. (*Let's see what new dish I can concoct today.*)

For some, food provides a format for self-care. (*I'm making myself a nutritious soup with organic vegetables.)*

For many, food is used to soothe — to reduce stress, anxiety, or boredom. Maybe we are aching for something we don't have or stressing about a situation in our lives and turning to food as solace or self-medication. *(What a tough day. I deserve pizza.)*

For some, food is a source of stress and anxiety. *(Will there be enough to eat? Am I eating the right things? Am I eating too much?)*

For some, food is an addiction. *(I can't seem to control what I'm consuming. I know I shouldn't snack so much every day, but I can't seem to stop.)*

Food serves numerous needs at different times in life. We go through different phases during childhood, in adolescence, in early adulthood, and later.

For example, a common pattern during adolescence and early adulthood is to dabble with different dietary restrictions. We might deny ourselves the ingredients and meals we love the most . . . then berate ourselves when we indulge in the items we've been restricting.

We can't change what we've done in the past, so let's begin in the present. How would you describe your **current** relationship with food? To what extent do you enjoy it? To what extent is it a source of stress? What portion of your day is spent thinking about food? What are your current eating habits? To what extent do you feel in control over what you consume?

If you are dissatisfied with your current relationship with food, know that, if you choose to, you can improve it. There are specific steps you can take to alter your food-related thoughts, feelings, and actions.

I'm a life coach and author of two dozen books. I've spent the last twenty years helping people overcome challenges and make real, effective changes in their life.

As a reformed emotional eater, myself, I've gathered, developed, and tested dozens of techniques to improve my own relationship with food. I've designed this book so you can:

- examine your relationship with food — past and present
- appreciate and bolster the eating habits that you find healthy, helpful, and enjoyable
- recognize and transform unhelpful, unhealthy eating behaviors
- identify the real source(s) of your emotional eating
- detect and change unhelpful, unhealthy thoughts and beliefs that fuel your emotional eating
- establish a new, healthy relationship with food
- learn specific skills to manage food cravings
- establish mindful eating
- monitor your progress and make adjustments as needed
- recognize and overcome resistance or self-sabotage when it arises, and
- overcome setbacks quickly and easily

Understand that emotional eating is a highly individualized challenge. It manifests in unique ways in any given person. Different approaches work for different people. Specific tools might be more or less effective for you at different points in time. I've designed this book as a guide so you can customize the solutions that will work for you now, given your current circumstances and preferences.

Let me be clear: this is not a diet book. This is a workbook for examining and improving your relationship with food. If you are contemplating beginning a weight loss program, I recommend you wait until after you complete the process in this book. You may find that you don't actually need a diet after all.

Ж

How to Get the Most Out of This Book

Designate a digital file, blank book, journal, or notepad as your *Food Thoughts Journal*. As you read this book, make note of examples, insights, and solutions that resonate with you.

Use your *Food Thoughts Journal* to record your answers and ideas as you work through the questions and activities in this book.

As you do, respond as quickly as possible, capturing as many thoughts as you can generate in short order. Be candid. There are no wrong answers. By writing out your responses, you will elicit deeper insights and you will generate more ideas (including some surprises).

It is likely that new ideas will occur to you after you complete an activity. Feel free to go back and add whatever new insights emerge.

It is up to you to determine how much you'd like to get out of the experience of working through this book. The more you put into the activities, the more you'll get out of it. The more you write, the more material you will have to find your unique path to improve your relationship with food.

Due to the highly individualized nature of emotional eating, I am including a variety of tools, techniques, and approaches to overcome it. I encourage you to test each one to see how effective it is for you at this point in time. Make note of what works for you and what doesn't. Know that if something doesn't help you now, it might at a later time in your life — and that it is included in this book because it is likely to help someone else.

It is also possible to use this book with another person or with a group. If there is someone you trust who also struggles with emotional eating, go through the process in this book together. Read each chapter and do the activities individually, then discuss your answers together (in person or on the phone). It is very powerful to compare notes and support one another when you are addressing similar challenges. You will gain each other's insights and the benefit of each other's experiences to enrich your own.

Note that the tools and techniques in this book are designed for people who wish to improve their relationship with food. However, if you are seeking to overcome an eating disorder such as anorexia or bulimia, this book will be insufficient to meet your needs. Instead, please contact a qualified professional for clinical help. If you don't know where to start, ask your doctor.

※

Your Current Relationship with Food

Let's begin by surveying your current relationship with food. What's working well for you? What isn't? How important is it in your daily life? What follows are some initial questions for your consideration, alongside some responses given by people interviewed for this book.

What are your thoughts about food? How do you think about it? How often?

"I'm pretty food-focused," says Joan. "When I wake up, my first thoughts are about what to have for breakfast. My first thought after breakfast is, what will I have for lunch?"

"The only time I really think about food is for special occasions," says Steve. "I look forward to going out to a restaurant to celebrate."

"I love food," says Gina. "A bit too much actually. I look forward to mealtimes. I eat fairly healthy . . . make good choices during the day for meals and don't usually snack during the day, but unfortunately, I snack in the evening . . . not all healthy choices (i.e., potato chips and popcorn)."

"I'm really happy with my relationship with food now," says Alice. "But it took many years and diets and ups-and-downs to get here!"

What are your beliefs about food?

For example, Doug believes that food is fuel and nothing more. Susan, in contrast, gives great care and attention to preparing meals. "Making good meals for my family is very important to me. I know they don't fully appreciate the work that goes into it, but I do it because I love them. I want them to be healthy."

What needs do you address with food? Do you eat for nourishment and/or energy? Does food provide other benefits such as pleasure or solace or celebration or reward? Do you eat when you are anxious or bored or stressed?

Joan eats when she's worried. "I can't seem to stop snacking when

I'm anxious about how something will turn out."

How do you feel about food? What emotions does it evoke under what circumstances?

"I love, love, love food. I love to cook. I love to eat," says Melissa. "I have to stay pretty active to be able to eat the way I do. I go to the gym every day so I can eat as much as I do."

Karl has a soft spot for his favorite junk food in high school — red and black licorice. "Maybe it's nostalgia," he says. "It doesn't really taste that good. It's like eating plastic. But I still buy it when I want a treat."

Consider your actions. How do you interact with food? What are your eating habits?

"During the week, my main concern is what is easy and what is fast. I grab breakfast I can eat on the run. I'll grab lunch near the office. For dinner I make the easiest thing I can," says Janice. "I try to prepare 'real' meals on the weekend but that doesn't always happen."

"Man, I love to eat . . . but I can't seem to make myself eat the healthy food I know I should," says Christine. "I'm happy to eat any carb but vegetables, not so much."

"My relationship with food is mixed," says Devon. "I don't go for seconds. I try not to snack. I have three meals a day. But my portions are too big, and I eat too many carbs."

"Since I snack at night and enjoy it, I try to eat only two meals during the day to allow for those extra calories," says Gina. "Not likely a good choice, but I enjoy eating this way."

Do you have difficult controlling the consumption of certain foods?

"I can't buy certain things or I'll overeat," says Mark. "If I open a package of potato chips, I'll eat the whole thing in one sitting."

Do you hide your consumption of certain items from others? For example, unbeknownst to any of her family, Sally snacks on butter.

How is mealtime for you? To what extent is it calm or stressful? How mindfully do you eat? Do you multi-task during meals?

"It's super hard to corral my family for a meal and there is always something else going on," says Jill. "If I say, 'No phones at the table,' they just eat as fast as they can, then run off to text or whatever."

To what extent are you a snacker or a grazer? Jill eats small amounts of food throughout the day. Doug eats three meals a day with no snacks in between. Susan aims for three meals a day, but often succumbs to afternoon snacks.

"Oh, I'm so bad," says Gina. "I eat nacho chips. Late at night. Even in bed!"

Also give some thought to particular food items. **What are your favorite foods?** What do you not enjoy eating? What do you tend to eat these days? What are your special occasion foods?

Joan adores pistachios, so she enjoys a portion every day as a treat. Susan tries to eat vegan for the most part, but she loves cheese so that's her "special occasion" splurge.

Consider your current meal preparation practices. What is working well? What isn't?

"My current relationship with food is pretty good," says Sabine. "I am a foodie and I put effort into making healthy, vegetable-forward meals. My favorite style of eating tends to be simple, peasant style or ethnic foods as opposed to the typical American diet — burgers, steaks, fries, processed foods, pies, etc."

"My biggest challenge is that it's difficult to change my cooking style totally when I'm cooking for other people in my home who want different choices," says Gina.

When Jennifer married a man twenty years her senior, she learned, belatedly, that he expected her to cook him three meals a day. Every single day. "I didn't know this is what I signed up for when I agreed to marry him." Jennifer does not enjoy cooking, so she conjures any excuse to go to a restaurant or order takeaway.

When Marianne thought about her relationship with food, she recognized that while she wasn't happy with some of her eating habits, she also had some positive, healthy habits.

> **MARIANNE'S STORY**
>
> Food is a big part of my day. I think about it a lot.
>
> I eat when I'm worried or stressed. I eat when I'm bored. I eat to "help me think." I snack between meals, pretty much grazing throughout the day.
>
> I do have some healthy food habits. I eat a lot of fruits and vegetables. I seldom eat processed foods.
>
> I love cooking so I prepare fresh food every day. I spend a lot of time searching the internet for new recipes.
>
> I don't have much of a sweet tooth, but chocolate is a favorite indulgence. Also, caramel. And licorice. Okay maybe a bit of a sweet tooth.
>
> My Achilles heel is definitely salty snacks like potato chips. My husband and I tend to reward ourselves after each workday with an assortment of junk food as we play a board game to unwind.
>
> Probably my least healthy food habit is multi-tasking when I eat. How ironic! Here I am so food focused — and yet not really paying attention to what I consume. Instead of savoring my meals, I chow down while preoccupied with a magazine, a computer game, or watching TV. These other things have my attention while I shovel food into my mouth.
>
> I guess that's another thing I need to acknowledge: I tend to wolf down my food.
>
> "Stop snacking" or "get control over my eating" has been a New Year's resolution every year for the past decade, but I never seem to make much progress. From time to time, I've tried a couple of changes that gave me short-term improvement, but I always seem to revert back to my natural tendencies before too long.
>
> I feel like I've been at the mercy of my cravings for decades. It feels horrible not being in control of what I eat. It's embarrassing.
>
> I'd really like to get a handle on this. I'd like to feel in charge of what I eat. I'd like to overcome my cravings. I'd like to stop wolfing down my food without really tasting it. I'd like to have a healthier, happier relationship with food.

YOUR CURRENT RELATIONSHIP WITH FOOD

Now it's your turn. What follows is a detailed set of questions to help you consider different aspects of your current relationship with food. Pull out your *Food Thoughts Journal* (page 4) or grab some paper and a pen. Clear some uninterrupted time to answer.

This is a *critical* first step in overcoming your emotional eating, so take your time. Respond thoughtfully. Be as detailed as possible. The more specific examples you can jot down, the better. You don't have to answer all the questions in one sitting. Work through the questions at a pace that is comfortable for you. Take breaks when you need them.

KEY QUESTIONS: YOUR CURRENT RELATIONSHIP WITH FOOD

1. Describe your current attitude towards food.
   - How important is it to you in your daily life?
   - When you think about food, what do you think about?
   - In a typical day, how often do you think about food or eating or meal planning?
   - What are your beliefs about food?

2. What role(s) does food play in your current life? *In answering the following, give examples and details.*
   - To what extent do you use food as fuel?
   - To what extent do you use food as a reward or treat?
   - To what extent do you use food as a punishment?
   - To what extent do you eat when you are stressed?
   - To what extent do you eat when you are bored?
   - To what extent do you eat when you are worried?
   - To what extent do you eat to soothe yourself?
   - To what extent do you use food to self-medicate?
   - What other needs does food meet in your life?

3. How do you feel about food? What emotions does it evoke under which circumstances? *Be specific.*

continued →

4. Do you hide your eating from others? Under what circumstances? Do you conceal your consumption of certain foods and/or beverages from others? *Give some examples and details.*

5. How do you approach meal preparation? What is that process like? Do you cook? Do you purchase takeout or meal kits? How often do you avoid meal preparation? To what extent is food preparation a pleasure or a burden? *Explain.*

6. In general, how do you approach mealtime?

    - What level of calm or stress is typical of your meals?
    - What is the typical pace of your meals? How slowly or quickly do you eat?
    - Do you express gratitude for your meals? If so, how?
    - Do you multi-task during meals? If so, what do you do while you eat?
    - To what extent do you focus on the flavor of your food? How mindful are you when eating?
    - Do you put your eating utensils down between bites?
    - Are rituals a part of your meals? If so, what?

7. To what extent do you snack between meals?

    - Describe your snacking habits. Under what circumstances do you tend to snack (e.g., time, place, reason)?
    - What foods do you tend to snack on?
    - How comfortable are you with your snacking?

8. Do you have difficulty controlling your consumption of certain foods and/or beverages?

    - If so, which are problematic for you?
    - Are there certain items that you avoid having in your home to reduce the temptation of over-consumption?

9. Where do you shop for food? Do you enjoy grocery shopping? What is your priority when buying food (e.g., price, quality, organic, calories, etc.)?

continued →

> 10. What are your typical meals these days? What foods and dishes do you tend to eat most often?
> 11. What are your favorite "special occasion" foods?
> 12. What foods do you not enjoy? What foods do you avoid?
> 13. Where do you like to eat out?
> 14. If you could wave a magic wand to create a perfect meal as your last meal on earth, what would you have? *Be as detailed as possible.*

When you have answered all the questions on pages 9 - 11, take a break. Wait until at least tomorrow before resuming this process. In the interim, if other thoughts occur to you, add them to your answers.

****

When you are ready to continue, reflect on your answers to this initial set of questions. What insights have emerged? What do you notice?

It is likely that some initial ideas will occur to you about how you might curtail your emotional eating.

Marianne resolved to stop multi-tasking during meals so she could focus on her food and eat more mindfully. She banned magazines, phones, and tablets from the table and made sure the TV was off.

Susan realized that she had a habit of snacking when she was surfing the internet. She made a new rule of "No eating at the computer." If she wanted to snack, she made a point of leaving her computer and eating at her dining table.

Gina saw that her nighttime eating was out of control. She set a "food curfew," committing to avoid eating after 7:30 pm. She set an alarm on her phone and brushed her teeth at this time as a signal that she was done eating for the day.

Steven snacked when he was stressed. He needed to find alternative ways to cope. He started taking a few two-minute meditation breaks in his day. If he found himself reaching for stress snacks, he'd set a timer and walk around the building for five minutes.

Jill realized she was being unnecessarily cheap when buying

groceries. She tended to shop for the least expensive items and denied herself more expensive treats. She decided to change that and started purchasing whatever items looked the freshest and best quality, regardless of cost. She found organic produce to be tastier and more satisfying.

What about you? Based on your initial thoughts about your relationship with food, what seems most pressing? What actions can you begin to take to improve your eating habits?

ACTIVITY:

1. Re-read your answers to the questions on pages 9 -11. Highlight or circle anything that seems important or interesting. Make notes as any new thoughts occur to you.

2. Answer the following questions in your *Food Thoughts Journal*:

- As you read what you've written so far, what jumps out at you?

- What patterns do you see?

- Any surprises?

- What are your favorite aspects of your current relationship with food? What is working well for you? What seems healthy and helpful?

- What are your least favorite aspects of your current relationship with food? What seems unhealthy or unhelpful?

- At this point in time, what is your top priority in adjusting your relationship with food?

- If you could make this change, what would it mean to you? How would it feel? What benefits might there be?

- What initial steps can you take to improve your relationship with food?

The preceding questions and activity have been designed to elicit:

- initial insights into the roles that food plays in your current life
- recognition of what is working well for you — and what is not, and
- initial ideas about actions you can take to begin to improve your relationship with food

Before delving deeper into your relationship with food, it's important to give attention to two topics:

- How to manage cravings (Chapter 2)
- Mindful eating (Chapter 3)

These are essential skills that provide a firm foundation to overcome emotional eating and to improve your relationship with food. When you implement these techniques, you will be on firmer footing to make real, lasting changes going forward.

Next, consider how you got to this point. Chapter 4 provides a guide to examine the role of food in your past. This will elicit new insights and generate new ideas to improve your eating habits.

Chapter 5 provides a process to identify your preferred relationship with food. What is important to you? What do you want to do more of? What do you want to reduce or avoid?

When you have a vision of your preferred relationship with food, Chapter 6 will direct you in how to implement your desired plans. It is packed with techniques to keep you on track.

Chapter 7 will provide specific ways to take good care of your body, mind, and spirit as you implement your plans.

Chapter 8 will prepare you for the likely resistance and self-sabotage you may experience as you make changes.

Chapter 9 will hone in on solutions to possible setbacks you may encounter.

Ж

Are you ready to manage your food cravings? If so, please turn to the next chapter.

Chapter 2

Manage Cravings

If you are someone who experiences food cravings that you find difficult to control, this chapter is for you. (If this is not an issue for you, please skip ahead to the next chapter.)

When you experience food cravings, how do they manifest?

"They are pretty intense. I just feel like ugh, if I could have something sweet, I'll feel better," says Devon. "If I could have a sandwich, then I can make it to dinner without being so hungry because I'm sad or upset about something."

"My food cravings are usually in late afternoon or as I'm prepping and cooking dinner. Not daily but a few times a week," says Sabine. "My cravings seem more related to emotions — boredom, frustration, maybe tiredness — than hunger. If lunch didn't have a protein component, it's more likely that I'll have a food craving."

"My food cravings can be triggered by the oddest things — not usually by a commercial or billboard or smell, but sometimes by an offhand memory," says Jennifer. "I may or may not give in, depending on what the craving is. Is it easily satisfied (e.g., something readily accessible and not forbidden by calories or diet restrictions) or not (something not readily available, like my favorite pizza from a place a thousand miles away)?"

"My food cravings are triggered by food smells, people eating, or just my stomach gurgling," says Stephanie. "My thoughts and feelings are: get out of my way! I need to eat!"

Take a moment to consider your own food cravings.

> **ACTIVITY:**
>
> Make notes in your *Food Thoughts Journal* (page 4): How do your food cravings manifest?
>
> - Under what circumstances? Any particular time, locations, or other triggers?
> - Do you crave particular foods?
> - How do they feel? What do you experience physically?
> - What emotions surface when you experience food cravings?
> - How do you tend to respond to them?

Food cravings are a part of human nature. You have experienced them in the past and will experience them in the future.

"Sometimes I feel guilty about succumbing to my food cravings. I judge my lack of will power," says Sabine.

Does that sound like you? If so, know that guilt, shame, and judgment are not helpful. They just make you feel badly about yourself, which can trigger more emotional eating in an attempt to soothe yourself. It can become a vicious circle.

It doesn't matter how you have dealt with food cravings in the past. That is over and done and unchangeable. But right now, you can press the proverbial reset button. You can choose to chart a new course of action.

It's up to you: Going forward, how will you manage your food cravings when they occur?

Whenever you experience a craving for food, you have options.

(a) You can give in. You can eat. This is a choice.

(b) Alternatively, you can pause and process what is happening. You can ask: is this real hunger or is it something else? Am I reaching for food because I'm stressed or bored or worried or trying to soothe myself? What is my real need here? Is food actually required or do I need something else? Based on your answers, you can make a choice to eat or to direct your attention and actions in a different direction.

Step one in managing your food cravings, therefore, is to differentiate between real biologically-based hunger and cravings that arise from other sources.

Ж

Recognize Real Hunger

Some food cravings are due to actual hunger. Many are not. Can you discern the difference?

Hunger manifests differently in different people, so it is important to know how your unique body signals a true need for food.

Some people are so afraid of being hungry, they never let themselves experience it. But if you don't experience it, you can't recognize it and you can't distinguish it from non-biological urges. Without understanding what *real* biological hunger is, you can't accurately process food cravings when they occur.

Try the following activity as an experiment. See what actual hunger feels like to you. Note: this might feel scary or uncomfortable so know that this is a short-term, temporary situation and that it is a key step in addressing your emotional eating.

Ideally, do the following activity now, then return after you have completed it.

ACTIVITY:

Starting right now, refrain from eating. Avoid consuming anything other than water for the next few hours.

Make notes in your *Food Thoughts Journal*. Chronicle what you are experiencing. What thoughts and feelings occur to you?

Pay attention to your body. What do you notice?

Be sure to stay hydrated throughout this activity. The goal is to learn how to detect hunger, not thirst or symptoms of dehydration.

Continued →

Overcome Emotional Eating

> Eventually, you will experience actual hunger. This feels different to different people so pay attention to how your body feels. Take notes in your *Journal*. Make sure that you can recognize hunger when it occurs — and that you can differentiate it from non-biological urges to eat.
>
> To conclude, eat something tasty and nutritious. Consume it slowly and mindfully. Pay attention to the flavors. Take notes.
>
> Then, continue your observation: how long does it take for your body to feel differently? How much time elapses until the signs of hunger abate?

****

If you did the preceding activity, congratulate yourself! It is perhaps the most challenging — and most important — activity in this book. Now that you can recognize real, biological hunger, you will be in a far stronger place to discern the nature of food cravings when they occur. *(If you didn't do the activity, there's not much point in proceeding with this chapter until you do. Feel free to skip ahead to the next chapter. Whenever you **are** ready to do this activity, come on back.)*

If you are like most people who do this activity, you probably experienced some surprises. It probably took a lot longer than you expected for you to feel real hunger. Your mind probably generated all kinds of fears and anxious thoughts in the interim. Your biological hunger probably felt different than you anticipated. When you did eat something, there may have been a tendency to wolf down your food. You may have experienced a rush of new emotions. It probably took a while for your hunger to dissipate.

This is all important information for you to process food cravings when they occur.

But first consider ways to avoid cravings in the first place.

Ж

Avoid the Cravings You Can

Some cravings are triggered by specific foods or times or day or habits. To the extent you can identify cues or situations that tend to elicit your food cravings, you can explore ways to avoid them.

When do you tend to experience food cravings? At what times? Under what circumstances? Joan tends to crave fatty, salty snacks in the late afternoon pretty much every day.

Ryan craves junk food if he knows it is in the house. "My wife bought a bag of chips for company and I could not stop thinking about it. I was obsessed. Of course, I ended up eating the whole thing."

Susan developed a daily habit of sitting at her computer immediately after finishing lunch to surf news websites. As she did, she would munch on nuts or cheese, even though she'd just eaten.

To the extent you can anticipate when you are likely to experience cravings, you can take steps to thwart them pre-emptively.

Joan counters her late afternoon urges by substituting carrots and celery sticks. She reminds herself it is only a short time until supper. She'll have a glass of water or cup of tea and busy herself with household chores.

Ryan knows he has to keep junk food out of the house. He asked his wife to help. If she buys chips or candy, he requests that she keep them in her car or office.

Susan wants to disrupt her after-lunch pattern. Instead of sitting down at her computer to surf the news immediately after eating her meal, she physically removes herself from that location by going elsewhere to read or meditate for a few minutes. She has been surprised at how easy it is to curb her cravings. "If I just avoid my computer after eating, I don't feel any urge to snack! What a relief."

Steve started drinking at least seven glasses of water a day for health purposes. As a side benefit, he found that his food cravings became much less frequent and less intense. "I guess when I thought I was craving food, what my body really wanted was water."

> **ACTIVITY:**
>
> Refer to your answers on page 16.
>
> Beside each item you've identified, brainstorm ways you might **avoid** these cravings.

※

Set Intentions

Another way to evade cravings is to set intentions. Start off the day by making it a priority to avoid emotional eating. In the morning, identify a few things you fully intend to do that day. Maybe choose your top work priority, your top personal priority, and something like "be purposeful in my food choices."

For each, priority, have a clear plan to make it happen. Chloe, for example, intends to circumvent her mid-morning cravings by walking around the block if the weather permits or by reading if it is inclement.

Another option would be to set intentions for your food consumption for the entire day. Many dietary programs make it a requirement to plan and commit to what you will eat each day. When you have a solid plan, you know what food items you will consume at different times in the day. It makes it easier to execute.

> **TECHNIQUE: SET DAILY INTENTIONS**
>
> 1. Make it a morning habit to identify clear intentions for yourself. What are the three most important things you'd like to do today? Jot them down on the left side of a page.
> 2. If it is not already on your list, add "be purposeful in my food choices."
> 3. Beside each priority, jot down a few ideas as to how you will accomplish this.

Do what you can to anticipate and avoid the cravings you can.

※

Interrupt Cravings When They Occur

When you experience food cravings, do what you can to disrupt them. If you notice you are reaching for food when you are not hungry, pause. Ask: how can I disrupt this urge? How can I nip this in the bud?

Consider the following six successful strategies:

- **Denial** — Tell yourself "No"

Some people find they can "just say no." They may say it out loud. They might make a stop sign with their hand to reinforce their direction. If you haven't already, try it and see if it works for you.

Kathy found wearing an elastic band around her wrist was helpful. When she felt the urge to snack, she said "no" and snapped the elastic. It hurt, briefly, and seemed to be enough to disrupt the urge to eat. After a week of doing this, she found that the frequency of her cravings had reduced considerably.

"If I can't eat, I just tell myself, 'You're not gonna die from missing one meal'," says Stephanie. "And I try to make peace with the feeling in my stomach and see if I can even enjoy it. Being empty. What works well for me is just being patient."

- **Delay** — Defer

Susan found she could tell herself to wait twenty minutes. That was often enough time for the craving to pass.

Steve reminded himself how much time it was until his next meal. "It's only two hours away. I can wait."

"The worst thing I can do is just give in immediately when I have a craving for carbs or sugar," says Devon. "If I can just put it off for a few minutes, I can usually avoid eating."

- **Substitution** — Consume something healthy instead

Cher carries baggies of raw vegetable sticks with her to munch on, as needed.

When she feels a craving coming on, Lynn finds that drinking a glass of water or a cup of tea helps quell her urge to snack. "I found some really flavorful herbal teas. It's like drinking dessert! They completely kill my cravings."

Sabine usually eats popcorn when she has a food craving. "It would be better if I measured out an amount of popcorn to eat rather than eat straight from the bag because it's easy to lose track of the volume being eaten," she admits.

- **Dental Care** — Brush and/or floss your teeth

One of the simplest, most effective ways to disrupt a craving is to brush your teeth. Heck, go ahead and floss while you're at it. Enjoy a mouthwash rinse.

"That's how I quell my late-night cravings," says Gina. "When I brush my teeth at 7:30 pm, I suddenly lose interest in chowing down on nacho chips."

- **Remove Yourself** — Change your location

Jill takes herself away from temptation. If there are snacks in the break room, for example, she avoids that space.

When Chloe craves food for no good reason, she walks around the block if it is nice. If it is inclement, she walks around inside the building.

- **Distract Yourself** — Can you do something other than eat?

When Ryan gets the urge to have a particular food, he tends to obsess over it. He learned that he had to get his mind thinking about something/anything else or else he would give in to the craving. What works for him was computer games. "I get sucked in and before I know it, an hour has passed and I've forgotten all about whatever I was craving."

Marianne finds she can distract herself with reading or jigsaw puzzles.

Sally asks herself: what needs doing? If she is at work, she looks for engaging tasks she can check off her list. If she is home, she tackles some domestic chore. "I don't really like housework but I feel good when I get something done."

What about you? Do you have any hobbies? What activities do you find pleasant and engaging? What can you get lost in?

Manage Cravings

> **Technique: Six Success Strategies to Manage Cravings**
>
> - **Denial** — Can you say "no"?
> - **Delay** — Can you defer?
> - **Substitution** — Can you drink water or consume something healthy instead?
> - **Dental care** — Brush your teeth. Bonus point for flossing.
> - **Remove yourself** — Can you change your location?
> - **Distract yourself** — Can you do something other than eat?

Bookmark this page so you have it handy when food cravings strike. Experiment to see what works well for you.

> **Activity:**
>
> 1. This week, when you experience food cravings, try each of the preceding techniques. See what works for you. Make notes in your *Food Thoughts Journal*.
> 2. Make yourself a reminder of the six strategies so you have it handy. For example, you could jot them down on an index card or Post-It. You could make a memo in your phone.

Ж

> **Sally's Story**
>
> When I'm stressed, I eat butter. Yes, butter. I use a cheese slicer to cut thin curls of butter from the stick. Sometimes I sprinkle extra salt on the curls. I can't remember how this started but I like the way it tastes and the rich feeling on my tongue.
>
> I'm embarrassed by this and hide this habit from my husband and everyone else. (No, Sally is not my real name.)
>
> I realize that when I reach for butter, I'm really wanting to reduce my stress.

> I know that eating butter doesn't actually lower my stress. It tastes nice and soothes me for a few seconds, but then it makes me feel guilty and embarrassed. It makes me feel awful about myself — like I have no willpower — so that actually adds to my stress.
>
> I need to find a better way of coping with stress.

Ж

Identify Your Real Needs

It is helpful to find ways to disrupt your cravings. However, to truly manage your cravings, it is essential that you process what is really happening. What do you actually want or need?

Are you actually hungry? Does your body really need food?

If so, make a purposeful decision to feed yourself and eat mindfully (More on that in Chapter 3.)

If not, why are you reaching for food? When cravings occur, analyze what you are experiencing. What are you feeling?

- Stress?
- Worry?
- Boredom?
- Sadness?
- Loneliness?
- Anger?
- Guilt?
- Happiness?
- Something else?

To what extent is your snacking actually affecting what you are feeling? To what extent is it improving your situation or your mood?

What do you really need in this moment?

- Are you trying to numb yourself or self-medicate?
- Is this your way of coping with stress?
- Do you need to soothe yourself?
- Do you need to find something to occupy yourself?
- Do you need some social contact with someone?
- Are you punishing yourself for something?
- Are you wanting a treat? A pick-me-up?
- Are you seeking a reward? Acknowledgment for some accomplishments?
- Is the source of your cravings something else entirely?

Once you take stock of what you are feeling and contemplate your real needs, what are your options in that moment? What actions can you take? As you do, consider the Six Strategies for Managing Food Cravings (page 23).

For example, **if you are stressed,** sure, you could snack. Or you alleviate stress other ways. You could take a quick exercise break. Or meditate. Or walk around the block.

If you are worried about something, ask: what actions can I take to improve the situation? Do what you can. **Any** action will feel better than simply worrying. If there is nothing you can do to change the situation, then distract yourself. What else can you give your attention? Is there anything around your home that needs doing? Is there anything fun you could do?

If you are bored, consider your options in the moment. What else could you do besides eat? What's pleasant and engaging for you? Do you have any hobbies you could do? Do you like to read or do jigsaw puzzles? Any creative hankerings? Do you enjoy puttering around in the garage?

If you are sad or lonely you could call someone. You could go online and chat with people on social media or groups you're a part of. You could find a volunteer activity that appeals to you.

If you are angry about something, can anything be done to change the situation? If so, take action. If not, dispel your anger safely, in private — yell, punch a pillow, take it out on the treadmill.

Then find a way to accept what is happening. It might not be fair. It might be unjust. It might be unpleasant. Acknowledging what is happening does not mean that you approve. It means that you are seeking to move on. Now pivot away to a new direction. What path or action can you turn to?

If you are reaching for food to **punish yourself** for something you did or didn't do, be purposeful. Understand the reason you are snacking. Then make a choice. Is this how you want to treat yourself? Sure, you could eat. Or you could take another action. Is there anything you can do to improve the situation? Are there any apologies or amends to be made? Maybe you are being unnecessarily hard on yourself. Perhaps what you really need is some pampering and self-care. Or a hug. Or a reminder of your accomplishments.

If you are happy or seeking to celebrate, be purposeful. Yes, you should reward yourself! How do you want to do so? With food or something non-culinary? If you **do** choose food, savor it. Avoid any guilt.

Bookmark the chart below so you have it handy when cravings strike.

KEY QUESTIONS WHEN CRAVINGS OCCUR:

1. What are you feeling?
   - Stress?
   - Worry?
   - Boredom?
   - Sadness?
   - Loneliness?
   - Anger?
   - Guilt?
   - Happiness?
   - Something else?

2. To what extent is your snacking affecting what you are feeling? To what extent is it improving your situation or your mood?

3. What do you really need in this moment?

- Are you trying to numb yourself or self-medicate?
- Is this your way of coping with stress?
- Do you need to soothe yourself?
- Do you need to find something to occupy yourself?
- Do you need some social contact with someone?
- Are you punishing yourself for something?
- Do you want a treat? A pick-me-up?
- Are you seeking a reward? Acknowledgment for some accomplishments?
- Is the source of your stress something else entirely?

4. What are your options? List the actions you can take.

5. Be purposeful. Choose what you would like to do.

"My food cravings were generally for sweets and carbs. They were comfort foods that made me feel good momentarily if I was feeling down about something and to anesthetize the negative feelings that usually had to do with the feeling of not being good enough. Sweets and carbs were an easy fix to fill that void but would be accompanied afterward with guilt for not having the self-discipline to say no which in turn, reinforced the feeling of not being enough," says Laurel. "As I got older, I gradually started to recognize how I was hurting myself and became very conscious of what I was putting in my body. I still love sweets and occasionally indulge and I am ok with that since I no longer see food as an answer to negative feelings but one of the great joys of life."

Another fundamental way to manage your cravings is to be kind to yourself. The better you treat yourself, the easier it is to handle food urges. (More on this in Chapter 7.)

Monitor and Reward Progress

As you take steps to manage your food cravings, it is helpful to monitor how you are doing. By doing so, you can:
- make any adjustments as needed, and
- reward yourself for any progress.

The simple act of recording your progress can be very motivating in and of itself.

"I put happy faces on my calendar for each part of the day in which I avoid emotional eating — morning, afternoon, and evening," says Susan. "I can see, at a glance, how I'm doing. The more ☺ I see, the better I feel. A row of '☺ ☺ ☺' days feels great. I can also see problem patterns when they arise. So, say I see a row of days missing my evening ☺. That's a flag that I have to give extra attention to managing my nighttime cravings. When I see the pattern, I can figure out what's going on and take steps to get back on track."

What would be an easy way to record your progress? Marks on a calendar? Emojis in your phone? There are a ton of goal-tracking apps available. What appeals?

Keeping track can be intrinsically gratifying but it's not enough. To truly cement new habits, it's important to reward yourself for progress. Be purposeful. What do you want to achieve, specifically? How can you reward yourself for doing so? What would be pleasant, fitting treats you could give yourself?

For example, Susan treats herself to a candlelit bubble bath when she has a week with 15 or more ☺ marks on her calendar. Note that she sets a reasonable, doable goal: 15 ☺ out of a possible 21. She aims for *progress* in quelling her cravings, not *perfection*.

When Susan has two consecutive weeks with 15 or more ☺ marks, she gives herself $20 to spend on art supplies. Three weeks of success means she's earned a pedicure. She celebrates a month of achieving her target by giving herself a "Play Day" to do whatever she wants, guilt-free.

The idea here is to develop the habit of resisting your food cravings — and to reward yourself for doing so.

As you proceed, know that the more you resist cravings, the easier it will be to resist future cravings. It's a form of physical conditioning. The more you do it, the stronger you will become.

ACTIVITY:

1. Choose an easy way to record your progress.
2. Keep track of how you are doing in managing your food cravings. Make adjustments as needed.
3. Make a list of pleasing, suitable rewards you can give yourself for progress in managing your cravings. Be specific. What would you like to accomplish to earn which treats?
4. Make a point of actually rewarding yourself for what you set out to do.

ж

Get Support

You do not have to manage your cravings by yourself. Consider any of the following options. Does anything sound appealing that suits your present circumstances?

- **Accountability Partner**

Do you have a friend or family member who has your best interests at heart? Is there someone trustworthy who would be really pleased to hear, on a daily basis, about your progress in quelling your cravings? If so, ask them for support in accomplishing your desired goals. Maybe send them a daily text to report on your progress.

Even better if they are trying to accomplish something that you can support them in. Let's say they want to walk more. Then, each evening, they could text you how far they walked that day while you report how you did with managing food cravings.

- **Coach or Counselor**

If you would prefer a neutral third party to help keep you on track, consider finding a coach or counselor. Often, the act of paying someone to help you reach your goals heightens your motivation to accomplish them.

- **Support Group**

There are free twelve-step programs such as Food Addicts Anonymous and Overeaters Anonymous. They offer group meetings in person, via phone, or online that provide ample opportunities to explore your relationship with food. As well, members are paired with sponsors for daily accountability phone calls and personalized support.

- **Higher Power**

Many people find it helpful to call on a higher power to quell their food cravings. Spiritual practices and daily prayers for strength and guidance can bolster one's resolve.

Ж

Manage Your Expectations

Understand that some days will be better than others. Some situations will be more challenging than others.

Focus on progress, rather than perfection.

Pay attention to what **is** working well for you, and savor that — rather than fretting about slip-ups.

Look at the Big Picture. How you are you doing, in general? Overall, are you managing your cravings better this week than you did last month or last year? For example, let's say that you have avoided emotional eating three days this week but yesterday you succumbed to a craving for popcorn. Rather than berating yourself for the popcorn, focus on the more successful elements of the week: You managed your cravings for three whole days! That's a heckuva lot better than you were doing last week, which is better than you were doing last month or last year.

Ж

Another key skill in managing your food cravings is to give your full attention to whatever you do choose to eat. That is the focus of the next chapter.

Chapter 3

Eat Mindfully

The previous chapter focused on ways to avoid or manage cravings. When you **do** choose to eat, you have the opportunity to make the most of it. A key part of improving your relationship with food is to appreciate it. To enjoy it. To savor it.

This chapter is for you if:

- you tend to rush through your meals
- you multi-task while you eat, and/or
- you tend to shovel food into your mouth without really paying attention to it

(If this is not your way of operating, please skip ahead to Chapter 4.)

Considering what it means to be "mindful." To what extent are you paying attention to what is going on in the present moment — as opposed to replaying events from the past or fretting about "to do's" or worrying about what might happen in the future? To what extent do you focus on one thing at a time?

Here is a quick activity to try, excerpted from Eckhart Tolle's book *The Power of Now*: Stop and monitor your mind to see what your next thought will be. Close your eyes if you wish. Be very alert, ready to pounce on your next thought . . . as if you were a cat watching a mouse hole.

Please stop reading and do the activity described in the preceding paragraph. After you've given it a try, resume reading.

****

How was that experience for you? If you are like most people, it takes a surprisingly long time for your next thought to materialize.

That gap? That time you spent, focused, waiting for your next thought to emerge? That's an example of being present — of putting your attention in the here and now.

That period you spent waiting for your next thought is mindfulness. It is a state of being totally focused on the present moment.

Mindfulness has many benefits: It feels good. You are apt to feel calmer and more like yourself. The more you can focus on the present moment, the more you can

- reduce stress
- avoid thinking about things in your past (none of which you can change)
- take a break from thinking about everything you need to do
- reduce anxiety about the future
- get more out of your experiences

If that sounds appealing, consider any of the following techniques to cultivate mindfulness.

1. Be

Take another break from reading to experience this. Sit for a moment and just "be." Clear your mind. Breathe. If you wish, close your eyes. For the next two or three minutes, focus on being here and now.

Please stop reading. Take a few moments to practice "being."

****

How was that for you?

Most people experience a sense of relief when they try it. When you can put your attention on just "being," there is no pressure. There is no stress. There is no regret about the past. There is no anxiety about the future. You don't have to do anything. You don't have to think anything. You can just be.

Happily, this technique is infinitely portable and doable. Anytime you wish, you can simply stop and just "be."

2. Mini-Meditation

The next step would be to make "Being" a regular part of your day through meditation.

The psychological and physiological benefits of meditation are many and profound. Almost every bodily system functions better when you meditate regularly. Meditation has been proven to be an effective remedy for stress, low mood, depression, and anxiety. For many, meditation is also a spiritual practice that brings solace, comfort, and meaning to its practitioners.

If you already have a meditation practice, wonderful! Please skip ahead to the next point.

If, however, you don't meditate, please read on. Despite all the potential benefits of meditation, what often stops people from giving it a whirl is the misconception that meditation requires grueling, boring and/or inconvenient l-o-n-g sessions. The truth is that you can derive all the psychological and physiological benefits of meditation through very brief sessions — just two or three minutes long — sprinkled throughout your day.

In fact, according to meditation guru Yongey Mingyur Rinpoche, it is better to aim for very brief mini-meditations than to tackle longer sessions.

How convenient! It's easy enough to take a two- or three-minute meditation break between tasks. It is not difficult. It is not complicated. It's just a matter of doing it. If you actually take a few brief meditation breaks every day, you will experience cognitive and health benefits.

If you haven't yet tried it, please stop reading and do so now.

> **TECHNIQUE: MINI-MEDIATION**
>
> Set a timer for three minutes.
>
> Sit quietly, eyes closed. Clear your mind. Breathe. Just "be." Gently push aside any thoughts that come up and refocus your attention on your breathing. Aim to think of absolutely nothing. When your mind wanders (and it will), avoid berating yourself. Simply clear your mind again. There is no wrong way to do this. Keep going until the timer buzzes.

Just as you can build bodily strength and skills by performing recurring fitness exercises, you can develop cognitive strength and skills by meditating regularly. If you do a mini-meditation, say, twice a day, every day, you could benefit every system in your body. The more you meditate, the greater the rewards. You are likely to feel happier and healthier and calmer. Try it this week and see.

3. Practice shifting focus to the present

As you go about your day, look for opportunities to shift your attention to the present moment.

What are things that occur every day that you could identify as triggers to shift your focus to "now"? This might be regular activities you do several times a day, such as brushing your teeth. If you drive, you might use stop lights or stop signs as visual cues to mentally, briefly, stop and be. Take a breath before you proceed.

You could use any phone calls or text notifications as a signal to pause and take a moment for yourself. When your phone goes off, pause. Remember you are here, now, in the present. Center yourself before you respond.

> **TECHNIQUE: SHIFT FOCUS TO NOW**
>
> Choose an activity you do several times a day, every day. Begin a new habit: whenever you do this activity, pause and center yourself in the present moment.

Be Mindful During Meals

The next step is to apply these techniques when you eat.

If possible, pause reading and try the following activity right now:

ACTIVITY: PRACTICE MINDFUL EATING

Select one small item of food (e.g., a berry, a raisin, an olive, a quarter slice of bread).

- Look at it. Turn it around and view it from all angles. What do you see? Describe the colors and textures you perceive.
- Feel it. Run your fingertip along its surface. What textures do you detect?
- Smell it. What scents do you notice?
- Touch the tip of your tongue to it. What is your initial impression?
- Take a small bite. Feel how it tastes on different parts of your tongue.
- Chew slowly and thoughtfully. What else can you taste?
- Put the remainder down. Take a slow breath.
- Take another bite. As you chew, try to detect other elements or features of what you are eating.

Cool, huh? Amazing all the sensations you can derive from just a small bit of food.

Guess what? You can do the same with your entire meal! Every time you eat!

Be honest: To what extent do you enjoy your food these days? What is a typical meal like for you? How calm or stressful? At what pace do you eat? What else is going on? Who do you eat with?

Where do you eat? Do you sit down to eat or do you stand over the sink as you munch on something? Do you eat lunch at your desk? Do you snack in the car or on public transportation?

Now imagine this: It's mealtime so you put away your computer, tablet, phone, and any other likely intrusions. Maybe you turn on some pleasant music in the background.

You sit down for a meal at a table. You take a moment to center yourself and "be." You feel gratitude for the food you are about to consume. You inhale the aroma. You examine the colors and textures on your plate. You take a first bite and put down your utensils. You chew thoughtfully and slowly. You give your full attention to what is in your mouth — the seasoning, the flavors, the textures. You take a moment to take a breath. You feel calm and content.

You pick up your utensils to take the next bite. You repeat the process. If you are dining with others, you chitchat between bites.

When the meal is over, you feel pleased. You've savored this pleasant, peaceful, culinary break in the day.

You then signal the end of your meal by, say, clearing the table, and brushing your teeth, before turning to whatever task is next on your agenda.

How does that sound to you? If it is appealing, start taking steps today to eat your meals mindfully.

If you feel that this would be impossible, that you are too busy, that your life doesn't permit this kind of indulgence, then I'd like to challenge that. Maybe you can't eat in this exact way for each and every meal . . . but you CAN eat more mindfully. You CAN give more attention to your food when you eat. You CAN eat more slowly. You CAN pause between bites. You CAN reduce (or hopefully) cease multi-tasking when you are eating.

Sure sometimes, you have to rush. There's no time to savor when scrambling to get the kids ready in the morning. Sometimes you have to grab a quick snack to fuel your body so you can keep going in the midst of a busy workday. Yet still, you have daily opportunities for more mindful eating.

No matter what your circumstances, you can:

- Feel gratitude for your food
- Slow down the pace at which you eat

- Pay attention to what you are eating — the taste, scent, appearance, texture
- Signal the end of your meal (e.g., clear away your plate and utensils, brush your teeth)

Consider this: the more stressful your life, the more benefit you will get from inserting some peaceful pauses in the day. Your brain and body need breaks from the psychological and biological ravages of chronic stress.

Why not use one or more meals a day as your opportunity to slow down, breathe, and be? Park your "to do's" and worries and concerns momentarily. Taste your food. Take a few moments to enjoy your meal.

Eating mindfully does not take *that* much extra time. Try it this week and see.

TECHNIQUE: MINDFUL EATING

Whenever you eat, try doing any or all of the following:

- Remove distractions and avoid competing activities. Turn off your electronics. Avoid multi-tasking while you eat.
- Sit down to eat. Ideally sit in a location that is designated for eating and not work or anything else. Rather than eating at your desk, is there a park bench or a neutral location available?
- Center yourself in the present moment. Avoid re-playing things from your past or fretting about "to do's" or worrying about the future
- Take a moment to feel gratitude for your food
- Pay attention to what you are eating — the taste, scent, appearance, texture
- Slow down the pace at which you eat
- Put down your utensils after each bite
- Pause and take a slow breath before taking the next bite
- Savor the opportunity to take this culinary break in your day.
- Focus on peaceful, pleasant thoughts.
- Signal the end of your meal. For example, you could clear away your plate and utensils and/or brush your teeth.

Ж

Mindful Snacking

Mindful eating is beneficial anytime you consume something — during meals and also when you snack.

This is the counterpoint to managing your food cravings (Chapter 2): When you **do** choose to snack, be purposeful.

What do you really, truly want to eat at this moment? Listen to your body. Does it want something cold, warm, or hot? Soft or crunchy? Healthy or sinful? Do you need protein for energy?

Know that when you snack mindfully, you will probably require less food to satisfy yourself. A teaspoon of peanut butter, eaten mindfully, will give you just as much pleasure as a tablespoon. Five potato chips, eaten mindfully, is infinitely more satisfying than chomping through a bag without paying attention to it (not to mention dealing with the guilt and shame of "Cravings Gone Wild").

So, when you decide to snack, make the most of it: Choose your snack with care. Select the portion you want to consume.

Feel gratitude for it.

Avoid multi-tasking while you eat. Give your snack your full attention.

Savor it with all your senses. The appearance, the taste, the scent, the texture.

When you finish your snack, take a minute to just be. To acknowledge this moment and what you have consumed. A snack eaten mindfully feels so much better than something gobbled down on the run.

TECHNIQUE: MINDFUL SNACKING

- Choose what you would like to eat, with purpose. What do you really, truly want to eat at this moment? What does your body require?
- Select a reasonable portion
- Eat mindfully (page 38)

Mindful Meal Preparation

When practical, you can also apply mindfulness to your meal preparation. Rather than rushing to throw together a dish or two, be purposeful: what would you like to prepare?

More importantly, why?

Besides considering nutritional needs, what else would you like to accomplish through this meal? To eat something tasty? To show love for your family members? To express your creativity? To foster a pleasant break in the day?

It doesn't matter what you are making — a sandwich, a pot of soup, a casserole, a four-course meal — let your purpose(s) for the meal drive your menu and the way in which you execute it.

Choose good quality ingredients. As you prepare them, focus on their textures, scents, and appearance. Taste your dishes thoughtfully.

As you cook, be aware of what you are feeling. Release any tension or judgment. Avoid worrying about if what you are preparing is "good enough." Instead, focus on your preferred purpose(s) for the meal. Aim for those corresponding emotions. For example, bask in the love you have for the people you are cooking for. Delight in the opportunity to create something new. Be soothed by the motions of preparing a nourishing soup.

If you are cooking with someone else, treasure this opportunity to spend time together. Have fun. Be positive and playful. Enjoy the opportunity to create something together.

Consider giving some thought to setting the table where you will eat. Maybe use the "good" dishes. (Yes, you can use the "good" dishes for a sandwich or pizza or anything else.) If you wanted to, you could decorate the table. Maybe break out a tablecloth, table runner, and/or cloth napkins. Light some candles or add some flowers. Turn on some nice music. What would be pleasant for you?

When you serve your meal, release any expectations. It doesn't matter what anybody else gets out of the meal, this is your opportunity to savor what you have prepared because you know what you have put into it. This is a gift for you, not anyone else.

Eat mindfully. Practice the techniques in this chapter. Savor what you have prepared

Make a point of designating at least one meal this week to be made mindfully. See what the experience is like for you.

TECHNIQUE: MINDFUL MEAL PREPARATION

- Choose your menu

- Why are you preparing this meal? What would you like to accomplish?

- Choose good quality ingredients

- As you prepare the food, focus on its textures, scents, and appearance. Taste your dishes thoughtfully.

- As you cook, be aware of what you are feeling. Release any tension or judgment. Instead, focus on your preferred purpose(s) for the meal. Aim for those corresponding emotions.

- Give some attention to how you would like to set the table. What dishware and glassware? Any linens, decorations, or enhancements? Would you like some music in the background?

- Serve your meal and release all expectations for how it will be received by those in attendance

- Eat mindfully. Savor what you have prepared.

⽔

Another element of mindful eating is to give careful consideration to what you are consuming. That's been important to Stephanie.

STEPHANIE'S STORY

My current relationship with food is excellent. I have a healthy habit of eating lots of fruits and vegetables. No meat or dairy. I have a garden where I get a lot of food from.

I ate really healthy all my life. Lots of salads and brown rice and

> vegetables. Smoothies and shakes. Seitan and rice pasta. I love to cook and am always experimenting
>
> I gave up all sweets for one year. Not even fruit.
>
> I fast usually one day a week. Sometimes I fast on just water, sometimes I fast on just one food. Homemade coconut yogurt with cayenne pepper is a favorite mono-food fast for me.
>
> The thing I do sometimes that isn't so healthy is I eat when I'm not hungry and sometimes I eat too much.
>
> I don't really ever crave anything that's bad for me. I know too much and I appreciate my body and health a lot. I have done so much work on this. I read books and experiment with different recipes. I know that I can recreate any "bad" food and make it a healthy dish.
>
> I'm actually grossed out by processed, preserved, chemical-added food. To think of eating an animal is repulsive to me. I know too much about how farmed animals suffer. They are given antibiotics to survive because their living conditions are so filthy. This is my major torment. Knowing how much harm animal agriculture is doing to animals and the planet.
>
> I used to eat cheese before I found out how cruel the dairy industry is. When I stopped eating dairy products about 16 years ago, my health improved tremendously. I stopped getting sick and having mucous in my throat. My face cleared up and I just felt better.

Ж

Chapter 1 examined your current relationship with food. Chapter 2 and this chapter were devoted to giving you some key skills to cultivate a healthy relationship with food.

Next, it is helpful to examine your past relationship with food to review how you've operated until now — and to foster new insights and ideas so you can make some purposeful changes, going forward. When you are ready, please proceed to Chapter 4.

Chapter 4

Your Past Relationship With Food

From the moment we are born, food plays a key role in our lives. It keeps us alive. It affects our growth and health. It provides us with different experiences. It shapes our behavior in complex ways.

By reviewing our past relationship with food, we can

- understand the roots of our habits and preferences
- identify long-term patterns
- recognize what has worked well for us, and what hasn't
- generate ideas about the relationship we'd prefer to have with food

Begin by considering your family's food history. Where and when your grandparents were born fostered their eating habits. What kind of food was available to them? Was it plentiful or were there restrictions? What roles did food play in their lives? What customs? Did they pass on any special recipes or traditions?

Whatever your grandparents experienced affected your parents' initial attitudes towards food. What did they then encounter as they grew up? What historical or cultural trends shaped their relationship with food? What food customs and habits did they pass onto you?

Pull out your *Food Thoughts Journal* (page 4) or grab some paper and a pen. Clear some uninterrupted time to answer the following questions. If you're unsure about the answers, ask other family members about their memories.

Overcome Emotional Eating

> **KEY QUESTIONS:** YOUR FAMILY'S FOOD HISTORY
>
> 1. What do you know about your grandparents' food history? Where did they grow up? What kind of food was available to them? Did they experience food shortages or restrictions? What roles did food play in their lives? What food customs did they have?
>
> 2. What do you know about your parents' food history? Where did they grow up? What did they experience? What food customs and habits did they pass on to you?

Ж

> **JENNIFER'S STORY**
>
> My American great-grandparents lived in a very localized world, either rural or semi-rural. Their food was mostly home grown or otherwise from local sources.
>
> There was deprivation during the Depression, with food scarcity and limited food sources. Obtaining enough food was a constant worry. If there were leftovers, they were saved and eaten.
>
> World War II brought rationing and huge changes for families, with women working and men gone to war or in wartime production work. Then when soldiers returned to the US, they brought back European influences they had experienced overseas.
>
> My grandparents cooked and ate like their parents did. Meals looked local and home grown. Then my parents cooked and ate much like their parents did, with some of the caution and rationing that had developed in the earlier generations. Big pots of food for family meals, leftovers, waste not/want not, etc.
>
> Then a little bit in the fifties and dramatically in the sixties, new kitchen appliances became available, as did processed foods and convenience foods. The opening of world markets changed the way most people ate.
>
> My parents still relied on some techniques and habits from a couple of generations past. But they then saw changes like processed foods, microwaves, and slow cookers. Remember the first TV dinners? They mimicked the meat and potatoes and vegetables and desserts of the

> earlier generational preferences. (They look awful now, but they were amazing then!)
>
> My children grew up with microwaves and instant foods and zero deprivation. They never had to worry about there being enough food and were baffled (and repelled) by my efforts to save leftovers. I didn't realize it at the time but they were probably ingesting a LOT of sugar and bad fats in all the processed foods we ate. It probably set them up to crave more of the same.
>
> I've notice that, now that they are adults, my kids rely on fast food and restaurants and take-out. When they do eat in, they either turn to frozen entrées and pre-mixed bags of salads — or they order restaurant food and have it delivered through an app. My great-grandparents would be appalled.

Ж

Next, consider your own food history. What have been your experiences with food so far? How was food regarded in your home when you were growing up?

"I had four siblings. We were expected to eat what was served, no whining . . . well you could whine, but it wouldn't have changed anything," remembers Laura. "We didn't have to finish our food — we just weren't going to get anything else. But for birthdays we got to choose the meal and the dessert that would be served."

"Women in my family were obsessed with weight and dieting. Very unhealthy relationship with food," says Alice. "I never saw my mother sit down and eat a real meal (unless at a restaurant) but the bag of potato chips would mysteriously disappear overnight."

"We didn't have much and we didn't have a lot of choices. We ate a lot of wild game: venison, moose, partridge. It wasn't really talked about. We were forced to eat what we were served," says Gina. "I didn't like mealtime and I didn't enjoy very many of our meals. Store bought sugary treats were few and far between (i.e., chips, gum, pop, chocolate bars)."

Anne remembers helping concoct elaborate desserts and appetizers for family parties. "Food was a treat. Something to celebrate birthdays or special events."

Consider your happiest food memories. What have been your favorite meals?

"I remember having pizza for the first time as a teenager and that was such a treat," says Gina.

Stephanie recalls "floating down the creek with my brothers picking blackberries in the warm sun and eating them. They were warm and sweet and it was fun."

"Every Sunday our family would eat out at the local Chinese restaurant, which was common for Jewish families in New York at that time," says Alice. "I loved the pu-pu platters, eggrolls, wonton soup, spareribs, etc. And the MSG always made my brother and me silly, although at the time, we never understood why!"

"When I was seven, my mom and I went on a mother-daughter extended weekend trip. We went to the zoo, shopping and ate in restaurants — a real treat because our family didn't have a lot of money. At one restaurant, Beef Stroganoff was on the menu. I had no idea what it was and asked my mother about it. She simply said, 'Try it, you'll probably like it.' I did try it and I liked it. I'm over 60 now and I still vividly remember that event and it always makes me smile."

Do you harbor any unpleasant memories involving food?

For Ryan, family mealtimes were a noisy, combative, argumentative thing to be endured. There was much jostling over who got what portions of which dishes. Everyone was expected to "clean their plate." Food was withheld as punishment for bad behavior.

"My dad came home with a fish he caught. I was maybe four years old. I saw that it was dead. I screamed and couldn't stop shaking," says Stephanie, who is now a vegan. "My dad had killed something that I considered a friend and now I didn't trust him."

Many people who contributed their stories to this book mentioned negative food memories about being forced to eat something unappealing.

"I was raised in the finish-what's-on-your-plate era," says Alice. "I never really liked red meat and some other foods and since I was forced to finish them, to this day I don't eat eggs and lamb chops. It turned me off from red meat entirely."

Laura remembers "having to eat what was on my plate even if I didn't care for it, like a freezer full of very boney fish. It took me a long time to like fish after that."

"My mom forced me to eat liver and I just couldn't keep it down.," says Gina. "I ended up vomiting."

Think about your early eating habits. Joan recalls being ravenous when she got home from school, so she'd serve herself crackers smeared with butter.

Susan made a weekly trip to the corner store to buy candy.

"Since I was a child, I've always saved what I liked most on my dinner plate to eat last," says Laura. "I guess it came from having to eat what was placed before me as a kid. And dessert wasn't a regular tradition in our house."

Your turn: Return to your *Food Thoughts Journal* or grab some paper and a pen. Clear some uninterrupted time to answer the following questions.

This is another key step in overcoming your emotional eating, so take your time. Respond thoughtfully. Be as detailed as possible. The more specific examples you can jot down, the better. Work through the questions at a pace that is comfortable for you. Take breaks when you need them.

KEY QUESTIONS: YOUR CHILDHOOD RELATIONSHIP WITH FOOD

1. What were your favorite foods during your childhood?

   - What did you enjoy on a daily or weekly basis?
   - What were your favorite "special occasion" foods?

2. What did you not like to eat? What did you avoid?

3. What early eating habits do you recall?

4. How was food regarded in your family when you were growing up? What words or phrases do you remember about food or eating during your childhood? What attitudes? What beliefs? What expectations?

> 5. What food-related memories do you have from childhood? Describe some specific examples in as much detail as you can. Include at least one positive and one negative experience.
>
> 6. To what extent was food used as a reward or punishment during your childhood? *Give some examples.*
>
> 7. To what extent was food used to soothe you during your childhood? *Give some examples.*
>
> 8. To what extent were you involved in grocery shopping or food preparation? What do you remember about those experiences?

****

If you wish, take a break. When you are ready to proceed, **consider the role of food during your teenage years and young adulthood.** What were your favorite foods? To what extent did you diet or over-indulge? What food-related memories do you have from these periods in your life?

Sheila and her friends tried various diets and fasts, vying to be skinny. Her typical lunch during high school was an apple. When she indulged in something fattening, like ice cream, she'd punish herself by not eating for the rest of the day.

"When I was a teenager and started making my own money, I spent some of my money on things I didn't get much of as a young child (i.e., french fries, ice cream and other sugary treats)," says Gina. "I got a bit out of control and gained about twenty pounds over three years."

As a track athlete, Karl was hyper conscious of what he needed to eat to maintain a certain physique and to fuel himself effectively for competitions. He measured his intake carefully and adjusted accordingly.

"I made a lot of food when I was a teenager. I loved to cook. I made bread and had a lot of avocado sandwiches. I ate really healthy," says Stephanie. "My aunt gave me a book called *Being of the Sun* when I was fourteen. I read it and wanted to be like the people in the book. They lived in a commune in northern California and spent their days growing vegetables, meditating and doing cool hippie things."

"I followed fad diets like the grapefruit diet and the Atkins diet, but overall, I could eat just about anything because I was very active throughout my early teens," says Alice. "However, my body changed around high school and I put on a few more pounds than I would have liked, so I tried to eat less junk food and fattening foods."

Junk food got Maria through her college exams. She was extremely nervous during test time and would chow down on chips and pizza as she pulled all-nighters to study.

In her twenties, Sherry had a vibrant social life — and food was at the center of it. She had a large family so there were many family gatherings that featured elaborate food preparation. She and her closest friends enjoyed cooking, so they would gather for meals quite regularly. These were happy, leisurely occasions she looked forward to.

Sid remembers the first time he asked a girl to a restaurant on a date. He remembers what they ate and how it felt to treat her to a meal. It made him feel like a grown-up.

"As a young adult, my eating habits were a mix between healthy and not healthy," says Alice. "I tend to like salads and other healthy foods, but stress eating led me to consume chips and ice cream and other junk food in excess. Bar food, too. Hey, I was single and going out!"

"As a young adult I still liked to eat treats but was making my own, somewhat healthy meals. I married young and cooked meat and potatoes most nights for dinner," says Gina. "Looking back, I wasn't educated enough to eat balanced meals and I didn't eat enough fruits and vegetables. But I could basically eat whatever I wanted and not gain weight so I didn't worry as much about my eating habits back then."

As a young mom, Betsy would finish off any leftovers on her kids' plates, lest it go to waste. (Instead, it went to her waist.)

Steve told me he gave his young kids chocolate any time they cried. "Oh, that's not good," he said. "I just realized I'm rewarding them for crying! That's not a pattern I want to continue."

> **KEY QUESTIONS:** YOUR PAST RELATIONSHIP WITH FOOD
>
> 1. Consider your teenage years:
>
>   - What were your eating habits?
>   - How was food dealt with among your peers at that time?
>   - Describe some specific food-related memories from your adolescence.
>
> 2. Consider your young adulthood.
>
>   - What healthy eating habits did you establish?
>   - What unhealthy or unhelpful eating habits did you establish?
>   - Describe some specific food-related memories from your early adulthood.
>
> 3. What food programs or diets have you tried, under what circumstances? What were these experiences like for you? How effective were they in getting you the results you desired?

At this point, you are encouraged to take a break. Wait until at least tomorrow before resuming this process. Should any other memories occur to you, add them to your answers.

****

When you are ready to continue, reflect on your answers to the preceding set of questions. What insights have emerged? What do you notice?

Have any other ideas occurred to you about how you might curtail your emotional eating?

Ryan saw that his hungry childhood years set him up to overeat even when food was plentiful. He had developed a habit of doling out huge portions to his family and finishing off every bit of food that was prepared for a meal, regardless of his level of fullness. He recognized his overeating was unnecessary, now that there was ample food available every day. He started reducing his portions. He learned to stop eating when he started to feel full. It was tough for him to get to the point where he could throw out leftovers. Eventually, he realized that consuming unnecessary excess calories every day was not worth the cost to his health and his self-esteem.

Joan realized that her daily 4 pm cravings for salt and fat were probably a vestige of her after-school habit of eating buttered crackers, two decades earlier. When she saw the connection, it became easy to deflect her 4 pm urges as false. She started to ask herself, "Am I actually hungry? Do I really want fat or salt?" The answer, most days, was no. Most days she was thirsty. Joan would drink a glass of water or a cup of tea instead of snacking and find that she was satiated.

> **ACTIVITY:**
>
> Re-read your answers to the preceding questions. As you do, highlight or circle anything that seems important or interesting. Make notes as new thoughts occur to you.
>
> - What jumps out at you?
> - What patterns do you see?
> - Any surprises?
> - What steps can you take to improve your relationship with food?

Ж

> **DEVON'S STORY**
>
> During my childhood, food was a reward. Food was an expression of love from my mom and my dad. They were both professional cooks — Mom cooked as a domestic, Dad was a cook in the navy and then had a BBQ place for a few years.
>
> After my parents got divorced, there were some hungry times. So having certain items were like a luxury. Most times we would have beans, rice, and cornbread. It was a luxury to have meatloaf or roast beef or baked chicken on Sundays.
>
> There were some happy memories, though. I remember going to a well-known breakfast diner. Not a chain. My mom and my older sister

Diana took me there for pancakes for my birthday. And the pancakes were so good. I was just going on about it. So, the chef came out and talked to me.

But most of what I remember is being hungry. Not having enough food.

In my teens I got jobs where I worked in restaurants so I pretty much ate what I wanted, as much as I wanted, when I was at work. And I was able to buy food for myself because I had money. I was able to make sure I didn't go hungry like I did when I was younger.

I was probably overeating but I didn't see it that way because I had been on the other side of that coin with deprivation.

As a young adult, I ate what I wanted, when I wanted it. I had a lot of years of eating expensive seafoods and steaks. I was probably eating too much rich food. And going out to eat a lot. Of course, I was gaining weight.

When I was young and vain, I went on every magazine diet — the cabbage soup diet, the Dick Gregory diet, and everything else. The diets worked. I would lose weight while following the diet. And then, I'd reward myself for losing the weight by going back to my bad eating habits. And gain the weight back.

I got to a point where I was looking to do Weight Watchers but I ended up contacting, by accident, an outreach person for Overeaters Anonymous. She told me about her experience in OA and it sounded like I would benefit from it. There wasn't a charge for it. You could give a donation when you go to the meetings. That really captured my attention because money was a little tight at that time.

The structure worked well for me. Structure included having exact food portions. Weighing and measuring my food. What also worked well was having a pretty strong support system in that if I was having some struggles, help was a phone call away. I was also attending meetings. Also, seeing people that were able to lose weight and maintain it for long periods of time. That gave me hope.

Because of the deprivation I had as a child, it was hard to weigh and measure my food and have the portion sizes without feeling like it was deprivation. It took a few years but I finally got over that.

> It was always a challenge to not have the high calorie foods that taste good. The foods I couldn't have when I was growing up because we were economically poor. To be able to have those foods and not eat them was particularly hard.
>
> I learned that the only thing that truly ever works for me is finding what triggers me and abstaining. Not having those foods. For me, sugar and flour are addictive substances. And once it's in my system, I just can't control it, so my best solution is to just not have it in the first place. Moderation has never worked for me. I can binge on anything. But definitely sugar and flour are my triggers.
>
> I know that I need to have some structure and a support system because left to my own devices, I find it impossible to not go back to bad eating habits and putting on a lot of weight.

Ж

When you think about your past relationship with food, you can identify what you want to continue and what you want to change. You can develop a clearer idea of the relationship with food you'd like to have, going forward. That's the purpose of the next chapter.

Chapter 5

Your Preferred Relationship With Food

Having considered your past and current relationship with food, contemplate how you would prefer to operate, going forward. Imagine that you had a healthy, happy relationship with food. What would that look like? In an ideal world, how would you like to approach your meals?

Ryan would like to get over his childhood worry that "there won't be enough to eat." Rather than wolfing down his food, he would prefer to feel calm during meals. He aspires to eat mindfully, savoring his food, and ceasing to eat when he feels full, regardless of how much food is left on his plate or on the table.

Marianne would like to overcome her habit of reaching for food when she feels bored or stressed or anxious or otherwise "off." Having developed a decades-long habit of soothing herself with food, she'd like to find alternative ways of coping.

Christine wants to eat healthier foods. She aspires to find appealing ways to eat more fruits, vegetables, legumes, and whole grains.

Joan had been approaching meals as burdensome chores that had to be done every day when she was a working mom. Now that her children have left home, she'd like to make meals more of a treat for her and her husband. She wants to give more care and attention to the dishes she serves. Maybe use her good china and listen to music when they dine.

Steve is motivated to be a good role model for his young children. He wants to help them cultivate healthy eating habits and to avoid

Overcome Emotional Eating

picking up his past unhealthy habits like eating junk food. He would like meals to provide opportunities for family conversations rather than being a time for computer games or texting or watching TV.

Clear some time to answer the following questions thoughtfully.

KEY QUESTIONS: YOUR PREFERRED RELATIONSHIP WITH FOOD

1. Imagine that you had a healthy, happy relationship with food. What would that look like? What would a typical day be like? How would you like your meals to be, in an ideal world? Describe in as much detail as possible in your *Food Thoughts Journal* (page 4).

2. Add to your initial answers. Consider:

   - How would you like to approach food shopping?
   - What would you like to eat more of? Less of?
   - How would you like to approach meal preparation?
   - Your preferred eating habits

3. What is working well for you now? What approaches, actions, and habits would you like to retain, going forward?

4. What would you like to change about your current food consumption or eating habits?

Now consider a reality check. What is actually feasible, given your particular circumstances?

For example, if you wrote, "Never snack," that's probably not likely to happen. Words like "always" and "never" can set you up for disappointment. A more reasonable statement might be something like, "I will avoid snacking mindlessly. When I do snack, I will make sure it is a conscious choice for a good reason." You might specify under what circumstances you find snacking acceptable, for example, if you are really, truly hungry or physically depleted or if you are joining a friend for a treat or if you are watching a major sporting event.

In the quest to help his children cultivate healthy eating habits, Steve realizes that, while he can make "family mealtime" a priority, life is apt to intervene sometimes. There might be some days when that is not possible. He knows he won't be able to shield his kids from junk food every day of their lives. But he can minimize their access to it in their home. He can model making good food choices. He can promote the benefits of avoiding empty calories.

> **ACTIVITY:**
>
> Read your answers to the preceding questions. Is anything unreasonable? Is anything written in absolute terms like "never" or "always"? If so, re-write it to be more accurate. Make conscious, purposeful choices that you know you can do.
>
> As you read your answers, choose your top priorities. What is most important for you?

Do you share meals with other people, such as family members or roommates? If so, get their input on the preceding questions. Meals are a communal activity, so it is important to know the priorities of all involved. Where are you aligned? In what do you differ?

For example, Joan yearned for romantic, elaborate meals with her husband. She won't be able to accomplish this if he doesn't find that appealing. She may have to compromise. Maybe he finds the candlelight a bit much, but he's happy if she wants to prepare more intricate dishes more often.

> **ACTIVITY:**
>
> If you share your meals with other people, ask them the questions on page 56. Brainstorm together. How can you approach meals in a way that addresses the needs of all involved? What are reasonable compromises?

⚜

> **ALICE'S STORY**
>
> I've refined my diet throughout my life. I had always been thin but gained 40 pounds in my twenties and tried many diets, none of which were sustainable (e.g., Weight Watchers, fad diets, Jenny Craig). I finally realized that (1.) I had to erase the word 'diet' from my vocabulary because as soon as I said I was going on a diet, I got hungry; and (2.) I need carbs to feel satisfied. I decided that my goal would be to try and eat healthy (rather than think of it as a diet) and try and weigh less at my annual check-up each year than I weighed the year before even if it was just 1-2 pounds.
>
> I always liked healthy foods but once I used the word 'diet' I felt I couldn't indulge without going off/ruining the diet. By changing my mentality, nothing was off limits since I wasn't ON a diet — I could CHOOSE to indulge or not at any time. That plus recognizing that for me, a carb-heavy diet (without guilt) at my meals keeps me satisfied so I don't go looking for snacks. Also, my family are cholesterol factories, so I had started watching the amount of cholesterol in my food because my cholesterol had started climbing. That helped reduce the amount of fat I was ingesting.
>
> It worked. Over the course of the ensuing 10 years, I slowly lost all 40 pounds and have never gained them back. My weight now has been stable and within the same 3-5 pound range for years. The biggest change was that within the last ten years I discovered that gluten sensitivity was behind my elevated liver enzymes, which had plagued me for as long as I can remember, so I eliminated gluten from my diet. It was surprisingly easy for me to do that. I found equivalent gluten-free products to replace nearly everything I was eating that had gluten. Unlike many people who switch to a gluten-free diet, it had no impact on my weight. (Most people lose quite a bit of weight.)

Ж

When you have a clear picture of your preferred relationship with food, it becomes easier to see what you need to do to make it happen. That's the purpose of the next chapter.

Chapter 6

Implement Your Plans

Once that you have a clear and detailed picture of your preferred relationship with food (Chapter 5), you can chart a course to move towards it. In doing so, consider:

- your motivation
- possible actions you could take
- your support
- possible challenges
- ways to monitor your progress
- possible rewards

Ж

Your Motivation

When embarking on a desired personal change, it is often helpful to assess your motivation.

    Susan wanted to overcome her emotional eating because she was tired of feeling like she was helpless to combat her cravings. She knew that by taking the reins, she would feel so much more empowered. It would boost her self-esteem to feel in control. She'd avoid feeling guilty or weak for succumbing to her cravings. She would stop criticizing herself and would feel so much better about herself. It would be a huge accomplishment to disrupt her unhealthy, decades-long habits.

> **ACTIVITY:**
>
> 1. Read your description of your preferred relationship with food (Chapter 5).
> 2. Why would you like to accomplish this? Jot down a list of reasons in your *Food Thoughts Journal* (page 4).
> 3. Imagine you could accomplish this. How would that feel? What would be the benefits? Brainstorm a list.

How compelling are your answers? Are you fired up and ready to commit to doing what it takes to reach your desired goals? If not, there is no point in proceeding at this time. Unless and until you are sufficiently motivated, you will not succeed in making real change. If you don't feel ready, put this book away until you are.

If you ARE fired up and ready to implement a plan to improve your relationship with food, great! Please continue reading.

> **TECHNIQUE:** MOTIVATION CARD
>
> 1. Copy your answers from the preceding activity somewhere handy (e.g., on an index card or Post-It; as a list in your phone).
> 2. Going forward, read this list every morning and anytime you need a reminder about what you are aiming to accomplish and why.

Ж

Possible Actions You Could Take

You know what you want to achieve — and why. How can you get there? What specific actions can you take?

If in doubt, think small. What are the easiest, smallest steps you can take to move in your desired direction? Be realistic. Aim for steady progress, rather than setting yourself up with unrealistically ambitious expectations.

As a way of eating more healthy foods, Christine had the idea of eating a salad a day, every day. When she asked herself how likely that was, she realized this was overly optimistic. Instead, she rephrased her goal by aiming to eat a salad at least five days each week. That was easy for her to do, less stress-inducing, and gave her more flexibility in accomplishing her desire to eat more healthy foods.

> **ACTIVITY:**
>
> 1. Brainstorm options. What small, specific actions can you take to move towards having your preferred relationship with food?
>
> 2. Read your list. As you do, edit as needed:
>
>   - What is reasonable?
>
>   - What is doable?
>
>   - What would be easy actions that you know for sure you would do?

Next, consider this: **Why do you think you haven't yet taken these steps to improve your relationship with food?** What has sustained the existing patterns you would like to change?

Your answers may reveal specific solutions.

For example, if you have established a long-term pattern of soothing yourself with food when you are stressed, you might explore other ways to reduce or manage stress when you experience it.

When Sally gave this some thought, she made a list of actions she knew would reduce her stress without turning to mindless eating. "I can take a break and remove myself from the situation for a few minutes. I can take deep, slow breaths and meditate. I can pet my dog. If I have more time available, I can go for a walk to clear my head. I can distract myself with a novel or a jigsaw puzzle."

> **ACTIVITY:**
>
> Take a few moments for some thoughtful reflection.
>
> 1. Why do you think you haven't yet made these changes you desire? What has sustained the existing patterns you would like to change?
> 2. Given your answers, what solutions might there be? What specific actions might you take to move forward. Brainstorm a list.

Ж

Your Support

As you contemplate actions you can take towards your preferred plans, what is already in place to support you? Consider:

- **What you know about yourself**

You have already accomplished a lot in your life. You have set goals, solved problems, and overcome challenges. When you reflect on your life, what has worked well for you? What hasn't?

Susan knows she is more effective when she focuses on one priority at a time. She realizes that rather than undertaking all her preferred eating habits at once, she will do better to tackle them one by one. As a new practice becomes routine, she will shift focus to the next item on her list of intended changes.

- **Infrastructure**

What things in your life are already set up to support your plans?

Gina is so busy, she rarely thinks about food during the workday. She realizes that it's only during the evening that she is tempted to snack mindlessly. It's helpful to reframe her efforts to focus on those four hours at night.

Alice has a dining table she seldom uses. As part of her plan to improve her relationship with food, she will make a point of eating meals at that table.

- **Social**

Who among your friends and families do you love and trust? Who has your best interests at heart? Who will truly support your endeavors? In contrast, who will you need to protect yourself from? With whom would it be best to avoid sharing your plans?

Be candid. Maybe, deep down, you know your mom will be a bit hurt by your efforts, as if your attempts to re-train your eating habits means she did a bad job of parenting you. Perhaps your spouse might become jealous — or worried that you are not satisfied with your relationship. Subtle sabotage can take the form offering you food you are trying to avoid. Or undermining your desired plans by saying things like, "Oh, you don't need to do all that. You look fine. Live a little!"

Next, consider what other support you might put in place. What can you easily set up to aid your success?

Ryan knows that it is much easier for him to avoid snacking if junk food stays out of the house, for example.

Also consider who else might help you in your endeavors. In Chapter 2, four options for additional support were described.

- Accountability Partner
- Coach or counselor
- Support Group
- Higher Power

Do any of them make sense for you as you implement your preferred plans?

> **KEY QUESTIONS:**
>
> 1. What is already in place to support you? Consider:
>
>   - What you know about yourself. What works for you when you set out to do something? What doesn't?
>   - Infrastructure. What is already set up in your life that will support your plans?
>   - Social support. Who will help you? Who won't?
>
> 2. What else can you put in place to support you?
>
>   - Do you want additional support such as those described on page 29?

Possible Challenges

As part of your plans, consider what challenges you are likely to face. For each, brainstorm possible solutions.

For example, maybe you are concerned about how you will navigate social gatherings while maintaining your preferred eating plan. You might take a moment before a social event to remind yourself of your intentions. Rather than eating everything on offer, you could decide to limit yourself to food items and portions you know are right for you. Whatever you choose to consume, you can eat it slowly and mindfully. You can drink water or seltzer during the event so you feel satiated.

Also, pay particular attention to how you tend to get in your own way. Think back over your past. How do you tend to sabotage yourself? How can you avoid this pattern as you implement your preferred relationship with food?

For example, if you know you tend to quit things prematurely, ask: what can I put in place to stop me from giving up before I establish my preferred food habits? When Susan did this, she came up with this list of options:

I will remind myself every day about the benefits of doing this

I will ask Debra to be my Accountability Partner

I will text her every day so she can keep tabs on my progress

I will give myself a reward for every week I stay on track

KEY QUESTIONS:

1. What obstacles or challenges might you encounter? Jot down a list.
2. How do you tend to get in your own way? Add to your list.
3. For each item you've listed, brainstorm ways you might address them, if they arise.

By considering likely challenges and pre-emptively brainstorming possible solutions, you are bolstering the probability of succeeding. Think of it as "inoculating" yourself from future challenges. By giving thought to possible obstacles now — and identifying possible solutions — you are less likely to be thrown off kilter, should these things arise.

Ж

Monitor Your Progress

If you really want to improve your relationship with food, you need to set yourself up to stay on track. This is where many people fail. They start, full of mad resolve and then, a few months later they realize, "Hang on, wasn't I supposed to be eating mindfully?"

You can avoid this by establishing routines to monitor and acknowledge your progress every day. Building on the ideas in Chapter 2, keep track of what you're doing to implement your preferred plans.

Give yourself credit for every conceivable victory. For example, you could give yourself credit for things like:

✓ *Reading your Motivation Card (page 60)*

✓ *Every segment in the day in which you manage your cravings successfully*

- ✓ *Every instance of mindful eating*
- ✓ *Every glass of water you drink*
- ✓ *Every mini-meditation (page 34)*

Visual cues are especially helpful. Stickers, symbols, or checkmarks on a calendar let you see your efforts at a glance.

You could take a photo of each meal, as a way of focusing your attention on what you are about to eat.

If you google "goal tracking," you will see there are plentiful apps available that you can download to your phone, tablet, or computer to set specific goals as you want and track your progress on each.

If you have opted for an Accountability Partner (or other support), clarify how they will keep you on track. For example, how and when will you communicate with them? What metrics will you share?

> **KEY QUESTIONS:**
>
> 1. What techniques have worked well for you in monitoring your progress in the past?
> 2. What else could you do? What might be simple, easy, fast ways for you to monitor your progress?
> 3. If you have an Accountability Partner or other support, how will you communicate? What would be easy and convenient? What metrics will you share? On what schedule?
> 4. Make a choice. How will you monitor your progress? Be specific.

As well, make a five-minute appointment with yourself once a week to review your progress over the past seven days. What is going well? What's not? What adjustments do you need to make, going forward?

> **TECHNIQUE:** WEEKLY PROGRESS REVIEWS
>
> 1. Choose a time that will be easy and convenient for you to review your week, every week.
> 2. For each progress review session, answer these questions:
>   - What progress have I noticed since my last review?
>   - What's working well?
>   - What rewards have I given myself for my progress thus far?
>   - What's not working well?
>   - What adjustments do I need to make, going forward?

No plan hums along perfectly, with no surprises, from start to finish. Every endeavor encounters some glitches and bumps along the way. It's important to be flexible in making necessary adjustments as you proceed.

※

Possible Rewards

Rewards work. When you actually give yourself treats for doing what you set out to do, you are more likely to make progress and stay on track.

In Chapter 2, you were encouraged to identify rewards for not snacking. Expand that practice to reward every aspect of your desired plans. If you haven't already done so, take a moment to consider what treats you'd like to give yourself for which activities or milestones.

Some of my coaching clients find it works well to give themselves points for certain things . . . then cashing in their points for fabulous prizes of their own devising (e.g., a pedicure, a massage, concert tickets, a vacation). For example, Sheila gave herself points for doing what she knew would help her improve her eating habits so she could "earn" new clothes.

Reading my Motivation Card - 5 points

Weighing and measuring ingredients for a meal so I know exactly what I'm consuming - 5 points

Putting my fork down between bites during a meal - 5 points

Eating a meal without multitasking — away from the TV, computer, or other distractions - 10 points

Doing a weekly review - 10 points

Every four-hour period without emotional eating - 25 points

If you tend to short-change yourself in this area — if you tend to avoid acknowledging your achievements — here is an opportunity to change. Try rewarding yourself. See what affect it has on you, your progress, and your motivation.

ACTIVITY:

1. Make a list of pleasing, suitable rewards you can give yourself for progress in implementing your plans. Be specific. What would you like to accomplish to earn which treats?
2. Make a point of actually rewarding yourself when you accomplish what you set out to do.

Ж

Start

When you have considered how you will implement your plans, **start.** Begin today. Take the steps you have chosen. Monitor how you do. Make adjustments as necessary. Reward yourself for progress.

Ж

Reality Check

You are in the process of making significant changes in how you operate. Be realistic. What can you reasonably expect of yourself, under your current circumstances? How can you set practical expectations for yourself?

Before proceeding, conduct a reality check. When you have attempted to alter your food habits in the past, what has worked well for you? What hasn't?

To what extent were you successful in the past? What interfered with your success? Consider any of the following reasons:

- You didn't have a clear picture of what you wanted to accomplish
- You did not include clear, easy, concrete actions you could take to implement your plans
- Your plans were overambitious
- You were not sufficiently motivated
- You didn't have sufficient support
- You knew what you wanted to achieve but never quite got started implementing your plans
- You neglected to monitor or reward yourself for your progress
- You experienced a challenge that derailed your efforts
- Your expectations were unrealistic
- You were too hard on yourself. You didn't treat yourself well as you implemented your plans.

It is essential that you pause now to examine what happened in the past. It is vital that you identify anything that interfered with your success, so you can address it this time.

> **ACTIVITY:** CONDUCT A REALITY CHECK
>
> 1. In your *Food Thoughts Journal*, write about what happened when you tried to change your food habits in the past.
>   - What worked well for you?
>   - Ensure that everything you list is a part of your current plan
>   - What didn't? What interfered?
>   - Be candid
>   - Read the list of bullets in this section. Which have affected you in the past?
> 2. Shift your focus to your current plans.
>   - Do you have a clear picture of what you want to accomplish?
>   - Do you have clear, easy, concrete actions to take to implement your plans?
>   - Are your plans reasonable? Doable? Are you 100% sure you can and will carry them out? Or do they need refining?
>   - Are you sufficiently motivated? Are you truly, deeply ready to make these changes in your life?
>   - Do you have sufficient support to implement your plans?
>   - Are you ready to start?
>   - Will you monitor and reward yourself for your progress?
>   - Have you considered possible challenges and brainstormed possible solutions, should they arise?
>   - Are your expectations realistic?
>   - Will you treat yourself well as you implement your plans?
> 3. Review your answers. Identify any adjustments you need to make to your plans.

Ж

When you have adjusted your plans, start. As you proceed, be sure to treat yourself well. That's the focus of the next chapter.

IMPLEMENT YOUR PLANS

SANDRA'S STORY

As a child, I enjoyed all foods and was an adventurous eater… hence I was never a small, thin girl, which sometimes caused me angst.

I tried Weight Watchers at some point in my forties. Didn't get any weight loss results from this approach and I found the point-counting a bit too obsessive.

Diets don't work. After several failed attempts at dieting, my approach has shifted to eating more of what is OK and hyper-focusing less on what I SHOULDN'T eat. As an example, over the last decade I have increased the amount of vegetables in my diet and I try to eat vegetarian at least two days per week.

I am more careful/observant about what I eat. When I asked my friend Michael how he stayed so slim, he said simply that he 'is very careful'… that got me thinking that changes in eating habits have to happen by choosing carefully every time we eat throughout the day.

The only significant changes I've made to my eating habits have been in later life as weight, cholesterol level and acid reflux symptoms increased. Intermittent fasting and avoiding cheese, red meats, sugar and wheat have helped to reduce the visceral fat around my waist even though my weight didn't decrease that much.

Getting accustomed to the changes described above took a few weeks to get used to. The changes in meal prep meant loading up the fridge & pantries with foods that were healthier to eat and avoiding buying the snacks that I used to purchase "for my husband" like cookies and chips. I read ingredient labels a lot when shopping these days.

Over-thinking about food/diet is not good. Better to go about making small, persistent steps in a relaxed fashion in order to change our eating habits. And, like meditation, we need to accept that wandering from our established 'food plan' is okay, it's part of being human. The act of re-starting again is where eating habits are solidified.

Chapter 7

Treat Yourself Well

As you carry out your plans to improve your relationship with food, be kind and gentle with yourself. Take good care of yourself.

Be proud of what you are doing. Realize that you are undertaking to change patterns of thinking and behaving that have been in place for a long time. They have worn deep grooves in the way you think, feel, and act.

Change can be challenging, so cut yourself some slack. Look for opportunities to:

- practice good self-care
- attend to your physical needs
- manage your mind
- reduce stress and cultivate calm, and
- nourish your spirit

Also, recognize that treating yourself well is, in itself, an effective technique to overcome emotional eating. When you treat yourself better, you curtail the need to soothe yourself with food.

"I was a terrible emotional eater for decades," admits Laurel. "I didn't stop until I learned how to be nicer to myself. Once I started treating myself better, I was on firmer footing and so much better equipped to handle food cravings. I got to the point where it was easy."

Practice Good Self-Care

To what extent do you take good care of yourself? Take a few minutes to contemplate how you are treating yourself these days.

> **ACTIVITY:**
>
> 1. What does good self-care mean to you? When you take good care of yourself, what do you do? Make a list in your *Food Thoughts Journal* (page 4).
> 2. Review your list. To what extent are you doing these things nowadays? Which are you doing? Which are you not doing?
> 3. What adjustments would you like to make? How can you do so?

Often, we signal our level of self-care through our appearance, our grooming, and our attire.

> **ACTIVITY:**
>
> Go to a mirror. Look at what you are wearing.
>
> - How well-groomed are you?
> - How do your clothes look on you?
> - How does your outfit make you feel?

What we wear can have a huge impact on our psyche, our mood, and our self-esteem.

Some people feel great in sweats or daytime pajamas. *So freeing! So comfortable!* Others find it brings them down. *Omigod, I feel like such a slob!*

If what you are wearing makes you feel good about yourself, wonderful!

If it doesn't, what adjustments could you make to feel better? Do you need to ditch those items that don't fit well or flatter? Would a brighter color lift your spirits?

TREAT YOURSELF WELL

That's the point of self-care: finding ways to feel good. This is highly personalized so take a moment to think about how you can treat yourself well.

What are your favorite simple pleasures? What are the little things that give you joy in your life? Are there particular activities that make you happy? Are there little treats you can give yourself to enrich your day? Is there music you enjoy listening to?

Julia buys herself a fresh bouquet every week. Matt treats himself to comic books (sorry, I mean "graphic novels").

Many simple pleasures don't cost a cent. Keisha's favorite indulgence is to take a nap. Paulo is finding joy in exploring online museum collections. Maria enjoys listening to certain podcasts.

ACTIVITY:

1. Think about your best friend. How do they treat you? What could you do to treat yourself more like your best friend?
2. How can you be kind to yourself as you implement your plans?
3. What simple pleasures do you enjoy?
4. What treats might you give to yourself?
5. What soothes you? How can you soothe yourself?
6. Who soothes you? Who can you turn to for comfort and solace?

Please make a point of doing the following activity today:

ACTIVITY:

1. What's one nice thing you could do for yourself today?
2. Make a point of doing it.

BONUS ACTIVITY: Repeat this every day.

Ж

Attend to Your Physical Needs

1. Practice good body maintenance

As you improve your relationship with food, take good care of your body.

Pay attention to how you feel physically. What is your body telling you? Are you stressed? Tired? Do you need more water? Do you need some time outdoors? Are you too hot or too cold? Does your skin need moisturizing? Perhaps you are feeling sluggish and need a nap or a caffeinated beverage. Maybe your feet are cold and you would be more comfortable wearing warmer socks.

If you are not sure, scan your body.

TECHNIQUE: BODY SCAN

1. Lie down and close your eyes. Scan each part of your body, putting your attention on one area at a time. As you focus on a given spot, see if you can detect any particular bodily needs. Take turns focusing on your left foot, left ankle, left shin, left knee, left thigh, left hip, right foot, right ankle, right shin, right knee, right thigh, right hip, groin, lower abdomen, upper abdomen, chest, neck, face, jaw, left shoulder, left upper arm, left forearm, left wrist, left palm, left fingers, right shoulder, right upper arm, right forearm, right wrist, right palm, right fingers.

2. Consider your body, overall. To what extent are you

   - Energized or tired?
   - Comfortable?
   - At peace or stressed?
   - Hot or cold?
   - Satiated, hungry, or dehydrated?

3. Ask: What does my body want right now?
4. Do what you can to meet your body's needs.

Ideally, develop the habit of scanning your body once a day. The more you are attuned to your physical needs, the easier it is to take actions to enhance your comfort and well-being — and the easier it will be to cultivate your preferred relationship with food.

2. Move your body every day

Regular physical activity is essential for everyone. Our bodies crave movement and our brains function better when we do. Physical activity is a proven mood-lifter and stress-buster.

If you are disabled, incapacitated, or injured, are you able to stretch or alter the position of your body? What physical activity is possible? To the extent you can move your body comfortably, do so.

If you are able-bodied and live a physically active life, excellent! Please skip ahead to the next section.

If you are able-bodied and not currently very physically active, consider how you might get your body moving. What would be fun and easy for you? Do you love gardening or yard work? Do you have access to children or pets you could play with?

As soon as you begin moving your body more, you will start to experience the physical and psychological benefits. It doesn't matter what you do, as long as you are moving your body at least fifteen minutes every day.

If in doubt, walk. Walking is easy, free, and can be done indoors or out. If you can't get outside, walk around inside your home. During the Covid crisis, for example, Justin Denson ran a marathon inside his Colorado condo. In Britain, ninety-nine-year-old veteran Captain Tom Moore set out to raise £1000 for charity by walking one hundred laps around his yard. Pushing his walker, sporting a suit and his military service medals, his efforts went viral and generated over £30 million for the National Health Service.

Physical activity is even more important if you spend most of your day sitting. Research has shown that those who do are inadvertently causing their body unnecessary damage. People who sit for eight or more hours a day have the same risk of dying as people who smoke! Many studies have documented the negative impact of a sedentary lifestyle: it slows metabolism and raises blood pressure, blood sugar, and cholesterol levels. It increases the risk of obesity, cardiovascular disease, and cancer.

The good news is that research has also shown that just sixty to seventy-five minutes of daily, moderate physical activities counters the negative effects of being sedentary.

If you are able-bodied, it is vital that you get up and move throughout the day. Make a point of standing when possible. Take stretch breaks. Find ways to move your body. Do what you can. Start with thirty minutes of movement per day. Ideally, work your way up to sixty minutes, seventy-five minutes, or more.

As well, consider what exercise options might be fun for you. If you love to dance, for example, you could take a class or dance along with YouTube videos or download a dance app on your phone.

What might make sense, given your preferences and circumstances? What fitness equipment do you have access to? Do you prefer to work out by yourself or would you prefer a live or virtual class? What options are convenient, given your location and schedule? Are there apps or devices that would motivate you to be more active? (e.g., pedometers, Fitbits, or training apps.) There are countless free fitness apps, YouTube videos, and online classes available.

Is there a fitness activity you enjoyed in the past that you are no longer doing? Is there something you haven't yet done but would like to try? Maybe yoga or tai chi or Zumba? If you research online offerings, you may discover appealing options that you didn't know existed.

HELPFUL DAILY PRACTICE: MOVE YOUR BODY

If you are able-bodied and moderately active: Make a point of engaging in at least fifteen minutes of physical activity every day. The more, the better.

If you sit most of the day, do more: Begin with at least thirty minutes of daily physical activity. Work your way up to at least sixty or seventy-five minutes a day.

If you are injured, incapacitated, or disabled: Find an equivalent activity that works for you. Move your body to the extent you can.

3. Foster good sleep

How is your sleep these days? Are you able to fall asleep easily? Do you wake up in the middle of the night? Are you over-sleeping?

Do what you can to foster good sleep. What works well for you? Reading? A warm beverage? A weighted blanket? A fan or white noise machine? Consider turning off your computer or tablet for at least an hour before bedtime. The absence of the screen light signals to your brain and body that it is night and time for sleep.

The worst thing to do when you have trouble getting to sleep is to start to fret about the fact that you're not sleeping. *"Oh no! I can't sleep! I'll never be able to get to sleep!"* If this sounds like you, the best thing you can do is catch yourself — laugh at yourself if possible — and remind yourself of a few truths: First, yes, a good night's sleep is important and yet you are perfectly able to function on less sleep from time to time. Yes, you'd prefer to be well-rested — but if you aren't, the impact of your sleep-deprived state is not likely to be detectable to anyone else. You might be aware you're not at your best, but others are unlikely to notice anything amiss.

Another common sleep challenge is to wake up in the middle of the night and have trouble getting back to sleep. Again, the fear of not being able to sleep makes it almost impossible to do so. If that sounds like you, understand that if you should wake up in the middle of the night, there is no need to panic. Did you know that, until about a hundred years ago, people practiced a natural "segmented sleep" pattern: They would sleep for a few hours, then get up in the middle of the night to tend to chores or family matters or pray or even socialize — then return to bed to sleep some more.

Waking up in the middle of the night is not a big deal. It's actually *normal* for us humans. There's no reason to lie in bed, tossing and turning, fretting that you've only slept for a couple hours. Instead, get up for a while. Savor the quiet. Do something pleasant. Read. Stretch your body. Meditate. Work on a hobby. Journal. Play with a puzzle.

Here's one caution, though: If you do wake up in the middle of the night, avoid the temptation to fire up your computer or television or another bright screen. The unnatural light source tricks your body into thinking it is morning already and then (a) you won't get back to sleep and (b) you're messing with your circadian rhythms.

Instead, why not use this 'middle of the night' time as a treat for yourself? You could use it to:

- indulge in simple pleasures
- attend to your body (e.g., do some gentle stretching, take a soothing bath)
- do some personal processing (e.g., write in your journal, make gratitude lists)
- nourish your mind (e.g., read, listen to music, work on puzzles)
- meditate or pray
- engage in a hobby you enjoy

Also, a warning: If you are having difficulty sleeping, do yourself a favor by avoiding chemical aids. It's such a tempting option: *Oh, something's wrong so I'll take a pill for it.* But sleep medications are fraught with side effects and health risks. They are dangerous when combined with many other substances. Worse, the more you use them, the less effective sleep aids become . . . so you end up taking higher dosages with commensurately higher risks . . . while you experience less and less effective results. (How many celebrities have left us too soon, thanks to these products? Michael Jackson, Prince, Tom Petty, to name a few.) Take better care of your body by avoiding these products.

ᏆᏦ

Manage Your Mind

As you implement your plans to improve your relationship with food, be aware of what is going on in your head. To what extent are you appreciating your efforts? Are you doubting yourself? Are you criticizing yourself? Are you cheering yourself on?

1. Cultivate helpful thoughts

Keep track of thoughts and ideas that feel good. Capture them somewhere you can see them when needed. For example:

I am in control of my food cravings.

Any cravings are temporary. They will pass.

I can eat mindfully.

I prefer to eat slowly and pay attention to my food.

I am proud of myself for improving my relationship with food.

The more I resist food cravings, the easier it will become to do so.

ACTIVITY:

1. Create a running List of Good Thoughts somewhere handy — in your phone, on your computer, in your journal, on index cards — whatever will work for you.

2. Going forward, review this list every morning and whenever else you'd like to refresh your mind with helpful, healthy thoughts.

3. Add new positive, helpful, or healthy thoughts as they occur to you.

As you go through your day, be on the look-out for other good thoughts. Actively seek ideas that give you strength and comfort. Maybe a stranger shares a helpful perspective that gives you a more positive outlook on your endeavors. Perhaps you have a new insight that makes you feel better about what you are experiencing.

You can also use your dominant hand as a reminder of some Good Thoughts. Try the following activity now:

TECHNIQUE: FOUR GOOD THOUGHTS

Look at your dominant hand.

Touch your thumb to your forefinger and remind yourself of a specific time you felt truly loved and cared about.

Touch your thumb to your middle finger. Recall a specific instance when you felt proud of yourself.

Touch your thumb to your ring finger. Remember a specific, significant way in which you've helped someone else.

Touch your thumb to your pinky finger. Remind yourself of a specific instance when you were truly happy.

Use this "handy" technique, when you feel stressed or need a boost. It's quick, unobtrusive, and guaranteed to lift your mood and shift your thoughts to happier, healthier topics.

As well, look for role models among the people around you. Who looks on the bright side of things? Who has a great attitude about food? To whom can you turn for advice or support? Who sooths you?

Be aware and appreciative of the positive people in your life. Gravitate to them. Thank them. Spend the time you can interacting with them. Learn from them. Emulate them.

2. Practice daily gratitude

Perhaps the simplest, easiest way to identify positive thoughts is to pause and appreciate the good things in your life.

It doesn't matter what is going on in our lives — there is always *something* to appreciate. We're breathing. We have water to drink. We have food and shelter. We have functioning brains.

Ample research has proven that if you look for ANYTHING about which you can feel gratitude, you will feel better. It will also reduce stress, shift your focus to the present, elevate your mood, and improve your relationships.

It's a powerful practice to express gratitude for what we have, who we are, and what we experience. It casts our lives in a more positive light. It shifts our focus to what's working well, rather than what's not.

Begin a daily practice of listing your blessings, no matter how small. (*I'm so grateful for the new herbal tea I found because it is delicious and helps me quell food cravings.*) Try beginning your morning by writing out five things for which you are grateful.

One caveat, though. Sometimes people try this practice and find that soon it deteriorates into a rote daily practice akin to writing out a shopping list. If you've tried this practice and found it lacking, do what Einstein did: Rather than just listing the things for which you are grateful, write out the reason **why**.

This small alteration — the additional explanation of *why* we're grateful — elevates and deepens each item exponentially. Rather than jotting down "my friends" on a laundry list of gratitude bullet points, it is much more powerful to specify the reasons. For example, *"I'm so grateful for Terry's call today because I feel loved and cared about."*

I call this practice Gratitude 2.0. I could list dozens of jaw-dropping stories about the power of the practice of expressing daily gratitude . . . yet the best possible examples are from your own experience. Do yourself a favor: Try it for yourself. See what happens.

HELPFUL DAILY PRACTICE: GRATITUDE 2.0

Each morning, write down at least five things for which you're grateful — and specify why.

"I'm grateful for X because . . . "

"I'm so thankful for Y because . . . "

Aim for at least five different items every day.

---

3. Counter negative thoughts

While you are cultivating positive thoughts, it is equally important to detect and counter negative, unhelpful, or unhealthy thinking. It takes some effort. It takes practice. But it is possible to learn to temper negative thoughts.

Much as we can try to avoid or limit our exposure to negative thoughts, they still sprout up. When they do, it's important to mitigate them. Process them. Work through them. Transform them into more helpful, healthier ideas that feel better.

Select one negative, unhelpful, or unhealthy thought that is currently on your mind. Work through the following process:

- **Consider the costs of this thought**

Let's say you catch yourself thinking, "I can't control my cravings." What is the toll of this sentiment? It's demotivating. It's depressing. It makes you feel hopeless — like a victim. It probably makes you cranky, which is unpleasant for people around you.

> **ACTIVITY:**
>
> Journal about the thought you've chosen.
>
> - How does it affect you?
> - What does it cost you?
> - What impact does it have on those around you?

- **Reframe this thought without absolutes**

There is a tendency for most people to frame negative thoughts in dire, exaggerated terms. If something doesn't happen the way we want it, we moan that it will "never, ever" happen and that "everyone" will think less of us for the rest of our lives. (*I'll never ever get control over my cravings! I'm doomed, I say. Doomed!*)

Does your negative thought include absolute terms such as "always" or "never" or "everyone?" If so, stop and rephrase it to be more accurate. For example, "I'll never ever get control over my cravings" is more truthfully written "I'm finding it difficult to control my cravings."

> **TECHNIQUE: REPHRASE FOR ACCURACY**
>
> Pay attention to the words you use. When you utter absolute terms like "always," "never," and "everybody," immediately rephrase your statement to be more accurate.

- **Dispute it**

Is this negative thought really true? What evidence is there to the contrary?

Identify facts that dispute the negative thought. The more counterarguments you can produce, the better.

For example, the thought "I can't control my cravings" could be disputed with facts such as:

> *I haven't yet found ways to control my cravings but that doesn't mean there are no viable solutions.*

Many people have learned to control their cravings. I can too.

I can control other cravings and impulses. I can find ways to manage my food cravings.

I have overcome other challenges. I can find solutions to control my cravings.

TECHNIQUE: DISPUTE THE UNHELPFUL THOUGHT

Dispute your negative thought. What evidence is there to the contrary? Write out as many ways to refute it as you can.

- **Generate at least three alternatives**

Counter your negative thought by thinking of at least three alternative ways of looking at it.

By examining other ways to view the situation, you are likely to generate thoughts that are easier to bear. They may be neutral. They might even be positive. They are likely to give you a sense of relief. To the extent possible, aim for an alternative that feels better.

For example, if you are reaching for thoughts that feel better than "I can't control my cravings," you might consider the following alternatives:

I recognize that food cravings are a challenge for me and I am seeking solutions.

I am motivated to find ways that work for me.

I can figure out solutions that work for me. There are steps I can take to manage my food cravings.

It will feel so good to find ways to manage my food cravings.

TECHNIQUE: GENERATE ALTERNATIVES

Going forward, whenever you notice a negative thought, pause.

Generate at least three alternatives. Aim for "neutral" or "accurate."

Produce at least one thought that feels better.

4. Suspend Self-Judgment

Avoid judging yourself. You are doing the best you can, under the circumstances. Be kind, gentle, and forgiving of yourself.

Consider your inner dialog. What is the tone of the little voice in your head? To what extent are you nurturing and soothing yourself? If you are operating as your own personal cheerleader, wonderful! Please skip ahead to the next section.

Or are you someone who tends to criticize yourself? Do you judge your actions? Do you tent to berate yourself for what you are doing or not doing?

If so, try something new. Going forward, when you notice your Inner Critic, quell it.

One way to do so is to actually write out whatever your Inner Critic says, then analyze each statement. Is it accurate? Is it valid? What evidence is there to the contrary? Might the opposite be true?

For example, if your Inner Critic is saying, *"You have no willpower!"* you might counter it with something like:

> *I have willpower in other areas of my life, so I know I have some willpower*
>
> *It's not a matter of willpower, it's a matter of finding effective ways to manage my food cravings*
>
> *If I had 'no willpower,' I wouldn't be taking steps to change my eating habits*

If you are aware of self-criticizing thoughts in your head, take a few moments right now to write (or type) what your Inner Critic is saying — and dispute each statement.

Then identify any thoughts you'd prefer to have in your head. For example, instead of *"I have no willpower!"* you may prefer to think:

> *I am learning effective ways to manage my food cravings*
>
> *I'm making progress. I'm doing better every week*
>
> *I'm proud of myself for taking steps to improve my relationship with food*

> **TECHNIQUE: QUELL YOUR INNER CRITIC**
>
> 1. What is your Inner Critic saying? Write down any critical or judgmental statements in your mind.
> 2. What tone does your Inner Critic use? Does it sound like anyone from your past?
> 3. What is your Inner Critic afraid of?
> 4. What is the impact of your Inner Critic on you? How does it make you feel?
> 5. Dispute what your Inner Critic is saying. Is it valid? What evidence is there to the contrary? Might the opposite be true?
> 6. What would you rather believe? Write out thoughts you would rather have in your mind.
>
> **BONUS ACTIVITY:** Post your answers to question #6 somewhere where you will see it often. Read it every day.

It is important to quell your Inner Critic because, left unchecked, it will sabotage your progress. We will delve deeper into this in Chapter 8.

Ж

Reduce Stress and Cultivate Calm

Often, emotional eating is triggered by stress. To the extent you can foster tranquility within and around yourself, you will make it easier to manage cravings, to eat mindfully, and to improve your relationship with food.

What do you already know about yourself? What are effective ways you reduce stress in your life? What calms you? Take a moment to remind yourself.

> **KEY QUESTIONS:**
>
> 1. How can you reduce stress? What works well for you? Consider actions, activities, people, and places that reduce your stress.
>
> 2. What calms you?
>
> 3. Who calms you?

If you haven't already, incorporate ways to reduce stress into your plans as you implement them.

Also consider proven stress-busters such as

- meditation (page 33)
- bringing your focus to the present moment (page 34)
- physical activity (page 77)

As well, consider these other simple ways to cultivate calm in your life.

1. Reduce unnecessary stressors

Some sources of your stress are unavoidable. However, take a moment to identify any stressors that you *could* reduce or eliminate. What are you subjecting yourself to that you really don't have to? What can you limit, delegate, or otherwise avoid? What could you pay someone else to do? What could you barter or trade?

> **ACTIVITY:**
>
> 1. Make a list of your current sources of stress.
>
> 2. For each item you've listed, ask:
>
>   - How could this be reduced or eliminated?
>   - What can be delegated?
>   - What could you pay someone else to do? What could you barter or trade?

2. Take breaks

Take regular breaks in your day. Five-minute mini-breaks can work wonders.

Aim for healthy, peaceful breaks — doing things that soothe or revive you. Stretch, breathe, or sip a cup of tea, for example.

During your mini-breaks, avoid unhealthy, obsessive, or stress-inducing activities such as cramming in a quick social media blitz or attacking some unpleasant domestic task.

> **ACTIVITY:**
>
> 1. What are healthy, helpful, peaceful five-minute breaks for you? (Make a list.)
> 2. What would be unhealthy or unhelpful breaks for you? Make a list to remind yourself.

Ideally, intersperse healthy mini-breaks throughout your day.

> **HELPFUL DAILY PRACTICE:** FIVE-MINUTE BREAKS
>
> Set alarms to ensure you give yourself five-minute breaks a few times a day.
>
> When the alarm buzzes, set a timer for five minutes and choose from your list of healthy, helpful, and/or peaceful activities listed above. Avoid the unhealthy or unhelpful activities you've identified.

3. Unplug

Technology takes a toll on us. Our minds and bodies were not designed to interact with technology as much as we do these days.

Studies have proven that the more time we spend completely "unplugged," the greater the improvement in our physical and psychological well-being.

For the past decade or so, I have advocated the benefits of taking regular "Technology Vacations." I encourage my coaching clients to spend a few hours — or a day — or a weekend — unplugged. No phone, no television, no laptop, no internet, no electronic games.

Kevin found great relief to shut off his phone and laptop after dinner. He found it fulfilling and restorative to focus on his family.

Teresa balked at this at first. She didn't want to be unreachable. She didn't want to miss out on the latest news. However, once she tried turning off her tech for a few hours every weekend, she saw the value in it. She used the time to do things that felt better. She puttered in her garden. She napped. She resurrected a long-forgotten knitting project. She didn't miss any vital phone calls. She felt calmer and healthier. She found that she could easily catch up on her email, voice mail, and the news when she turned her technology back on. In fact, she now makes it a regular practice to spend each Saturday unplugged.

To the extent you can remove yourself from technology altogether, for whatever period of time you can, you will reduce stress.

HELPFUL WEEKLY PRACTICE: UNPLUG

Designate a technology-free period of time for yourself each week.

For whatever period of time you choose — an afternoon, a day or more — turn off your computer, phone, electronic games, etc.

While you're unplugged, consider this next remedy.

4. Spend time in nature

Another proven stress-buster is to go outdoors. Our bodies crave fresh air and sunshine. Any time you can spend in nature works wonders in reducing anxiety and fostering health. How can you spend time outside?

If you live in a rural area, this is relatively easy. Just make a point of spending some time outside every day. Studies have shown that just five minutes outdoors is a mood-lifter.

If you don't live in a rural area, challenge yourself to find creative solutions. Can you walk around the neighborhood? Do you have access to parks or pets or gardens or window boxes anywhere? Do you have access to a porch where you can sit in the sun for a while? Can you open a window to breathe in fresh air?

If you can't get outside, can you trick your body into thinking that you are? For example, can you try a light therapy lamp or swap some light bulbs for full spectrum versions that mimic sunlight?

5. Relax

Most people carry tension in their body without realizing it. An easy stress-reducing technique is to scan your body systematically and physically release any tension you detect. (This is similar to the Body Scan technique on page 76 but here the focus is on identifying and releasing stress.)

TECHNIQUE: SYSTEMATIC RELAXATION

Clear a few minutes. Scan each part of your body, putting your attention on one area at a time. As you focus on a given spot, notice the level of tension in that area, then release any you detect.

Take turns focusing on and relaxing your left foot, left ankle, left shin, left knee, left thigh, left hip, right foot, right ankle, right shin, right knee, right thigh, right hip, groin, lower abdomen, upper abdomen, chest, neck, face, jaw, left shoulder, left upper arm, left forearm, left wrist, left palm, left fingers, right shoulder, right upper arm, right forearm, right wrist, right palm, right fingers.

When you detect an area under stress, place your hand on it. Breathe slowly and deeply. Physically relax. Imagine that you are releasing this tension out of your body. Keep focusing on relaxing this area of your body until you detect some relief.

Continue scanning your body. When you find another area of tension, place your hand there. Breathe slowly and deeply. Relax and release.

During periods in which you are experiencing chronic stress, you can use this method as an ongoing practice, once or more a day.

Attend to Your Spiritual Needs

1. Nourish your spirit

By "spirit", I mean that part of you, deep down that is your core inner being. It's your consciousness. It's the unknown forces within that inspire and guide you. It's your soul.

This might include:

- praying
- meditating (page 33)
- spending time in nature (page 90)
- expressing daily gratitude (page 82)
- reading inspirational texts
- listening to inspirational songs or speakers
- participating in groups or organizations that you find spiritually fulfilling

Which spiritual practices are already in your life? Which help you cope when you feel overwhelmed or angry or frightened?

In addition to your current spiritual practices, consider things you've done in the past that you found soothing as well as new ideas you haven't yet tried but would like to learn more about.

2. Seek solace and strength in your spiritual beliefs

It can be challenging to make changes — even good changes such as improving your relationship with food. It can be scary and frustrating to go it alone. However, many people find support and comfort by considering the larger context and convictions of their faith.

Journal about your spiritual beliefs. Write down what you know to be true. What can you hold onto as you implement your plans? What burdens can you release to a higher power?

SABINE'S STORY

Food was a central theme at home because my Austrian father and Italian mother were all about it. That said, his nostalgic memories of Austrian cuisine ruled what she cooked.

Dad was very food-focused and it seemed to represent one aspect of his life that made him feel content.

Meals were not complicated or exotic; just simple peasant-style foods including a protein (generally chicken or fish), veggies and some starch. No desserts were served except maybe fruit or ice cream.

When we visited extended family in Buenos Aires, meals would last for hours and include lots of talking, story-telling and even singing ... a very different experience than what we had in the USA.

My favorite childhood food memories are of Mom always making me lemon cake with lemon icing for my birthday, as requested. Also, the meals my mom prepared on the Coleman stove when we camped our way across the USA.

I also loved the opportunity to eat at non-American style restaurants in the 1960s-1970s because my parents were always curious: Greek, Chinese, Ethiopian, German, Italian, Mexican, French, etc.

My brother only ate fried chicken, Sloppy Joes, and grilled cheese sandwiches for a number of years, which caused great consternation for my non-American parents. I recall my mother plugging his nose to force feed him peas once because she was so exasperated with him not eating any vegetables.

When I was a teenager I ate savory snacks, M&Ms and McDonald's food probably due to elevated levels of hormones as well as the munchies after getting stoned in my late teens. The McDonald's food was a weird habit that my high school friends got into ... McD's after partying on weekend nights. Yuck.

My emotional eating habits kicked in with increased anxiety/frustration/whatever else related to growing up and pressures at university.

I spent several years as a vegetarian once I got to university but it was not done well. I ate too much cheese and too many processed carbs in

> order to feel full and ended up being the heaviest weight of all my life.
>
> My biggest eating issue is snacking between meals.
>
> Now I have some healthy eating habits, like Intermittent Fasting: I try to eat only between 11 am and 7 pm. I follow a Mediterranean diet. Lots of vegetables, simple dressings and sauces with less protein on the plate. I try to eat "clean" by avoiding processed foods. I eat very little red meat and minimize wheat products, dairy, and sugar. I have some fiber and probiotics every day (kefir or sauerkraut or kimchi).
>
> But, if I'm honest, I cheat on my preferred plan. I love cheese, especially goat cheese. I do eat sugar many days after dinner — usually a piece of chocolate. I'm sure I don't eat enough legumes or whole grains.

Ж

If you've been following the process in this book, you've identified your preferred relationship with food (Chapter 5), implemented plans to make it happen (Chapter 6) and are treating yourself well as you do (Chapter 7). The other key to overcoming emotional eating is to understand your natural resistance to change and to overcome it. That's the purpose of the next chapter.

Chapter 8

Prepare for Change

When you begin to implement your plans for your preferred relationship with food, you are likely to be highly motivated. You are ready to make this change and committed to doing so.

And yet. And yet, as much as you want to make these changes, you may find it challenging. You might struggle. You might encounter unexpected resistance.

In coaching people over the past two decades, I've witnessed that whenever **anyone** sets out to accomplish their desired plans, their most challenging obstacles come from within. It is natural to resist change — even good changes we really want to make.

Resistance takes many forms. Consider if any of the following are true for you:

- laziness (*I just don't feel like doing this right now*)

- confusion (*I just don't get this; This is too complicated*)

- excessive thirst for information (*I can't start this until I do another month of research*)

- overcomplicating matters (*Let me generate a thousand "what if's" and complications for any scenario; The solution can't be this simple — how can I layer in some other elements?*)

- fatigue (*I don't have the energy to tackle this; I need a nap*)

- deferral (*I'll get around to this later/ tomorrow/ someday*)

- excessive busy-ness (*I don't have time to do this; I've got too much going on*)

- scattered efforts (*Gosh I better do X — no Y! No Z!*)

- easily distracted (*Squirrel!*)

- self-doubt (*I'm not good enough; I can't do this*)

- worry, dread, or fear of the future (*What's going to happen?!*)

- self-deprecation (*I don't deserve to succeed in this; I'm too young/old/stupid/serious/goofy/[fill in the blank] to do this*)

- avoidance (*I'll just check my Facebook/email/phone messages; Hey look at this cat on YouTube; I really should clean the kitchen; Let me just see what's on TV*)

- impatience (*Man, this is taking forever*)

- perfectionism (*This isn't good enough; If I'm not executing my plans perfectly, I'm failing*)

- despair (*What's the point? This is too difficult. I'll never make this better*)

- self-medication (*Pass the tequila; Don't mind me as I shovel this bowl of popcorn down my gullet*)

- quitting (*Ah, what's the point? I'll just pack it in*)

Each of us has our own preferred, well-practiced ways of resisting, cultivated over a lifetime of experiences. You know yourself best. How do you tend to sabotage yourself?

ACTIVITY:

Re-read the preceding list. Use your *Food Thoughts Journal* (page 4) to make notes. Highlight whatever is true for you.

- What are your favorite forms of resistance?
- How do you tend to sabotage yourself?

In Chapter 7, we discussed ways to quell your Inner Critic. But sometimes what's operating is more invasive and nefarious.

Do you have a little voice inside that causes you harm? Do you have an inner saboteur that makes you doubt yourself, derail your progress, and/or otherwise create obstacles in your life? If so, join the club.

Everyone — no matter how smart or successful — EVERYONE has one (or more) little tyrants inside of them that cause them to do things against their best interests.

No matter what form your Inner Saboteur takes, the effect is the same: Resistance to change.

This is perfectly natural. When you commit to change, your brain tends to object. Your brain means well. It is trying to protect you from harm. Deep down, your subconscious mind perceives any change — even a positive change — to be threatening and dangerous at first.

That's why change so often sparks a random blend of emotions (e.g., fear, elation, grief, excitement, and more). That's why your clever brain will seek ingenious ways to sabotage your progress: it is trying to protect you from potential harm.

You can be full of mad resolve to do something, but if your brain decides to put the brakes on, it can be sneaky. You may find yourself procrastinating or avoiding something you actually want to do. You may find yourself acting counter to your own best interests for no apparent reason.

The solution is to

(a) recognize resistance when it occurs

(b) deal with it, and

(c) be on the lookout for signs of self-sabotage going forward.

In my coaching practice, I've found that the most common Inner Saboteurs are these five: The Fear Monger, The Delayer, The Judge, The Distractor, and The Quitter. As you read the following descriptions, see if any of them seem familiar.

The Fear Monger

Anything new is scary to this Inner Saboteur. Any change — even a good change — is regarded with anxiety and caution.

On the plus side, The Fear Monger keeps us physically safe and prevents us from taking wild, dangerous risks.

On the down side, The Fear Monger keeps us riddled with doubts and insecurities. It keeps us questioning our pursuits, rather than enjoying them. The Fear Monger sucks all the joy out of our plans. It keeps us paralyzed, fearing the future, rather than taking concrete actions today. (*What if this doesn't work? What will happen? Will I be doomed to suffer food cravings for the rest of my life?*) As well, the Fear Monger is concerned about "them" and what "they" will say. (*What will my colleagues say if they know I have a problem with food cravings?*)

Also, The Fear Monger makes us demand constant reassurance from our friends, families, and colleagues. This can make us draining and unpleasant to be around.

The Delayer

Perhaps the cleverest Inner Saboteur, The Delayer can find untold impediments to block our progress. Symptoms may include a sudden urge to do chores. Or eat. Or nap. Or do more research. Or walk the dogs. Or surf the 'net. Or check Instagram.

The Delayer impedes our decision making. We find ourselves hesitating to commit to a particular choice or option, let alone take action along a particular path. (*I'll start my food plan soon. But first I need to choose between paleo, vegan, and Blue Zones. Hmm. I better learn more about each before I can commit.*)

The less we do, sadly, the more frustrated and unhappy we become. We berate ourselves. We feel weak and ineffective. We think poorly of ourselves. This is heartbreaking for the people who care about us.

The Delayer makes us undependable, difficult to work with, and often tardy. This has an impact on most of our relationships, personal and professional.

The Judge

The Judge is rarely satisfied. No matter what we do, our inner Judge knows we could have done it better. It's the voice in our heads intoning, "This is not good enough."

Ironically, those of us ruled by The Judge tend to be plenty good enough. Because The Judge is picky and has sky-high standards, we tend to be conscientious, hard-working, and brilliant.

The downside is that we do so by putting tremendous stress on ourselves and those around us. We assess every situation, every person, and every single thing we experience. We work frantically and joylessly, and seldom pause to acknowledge our accomplishments. We are chronically dissatisfied with ourselves and with everything we experience.

The people around us find it uncomfortable to share with us, knowing that we are apt to assess and critique them and their efforts.

When it comes to food plans, The Judge insists on perfection. If our execution of our plans is less than flawless, it is perceived to be a catastrophe. (*I ate a cookie at lunchtime. Weakling! My food plan is doomed! I have to start over tomorrow and aim to 'eat clean' every single day. Any day I don't is an utter failure.*)

The Distractor

This Inner Saboteur is adept at finding cool new things to dangle in front of us. We just get going on a particular food plan when, suddenly, we are made aware of something new that hooks our interest. (This is also known as Bright Shiny Object Syndrome.) The Distractor is a master at scattering our efforts in random directions so we don't make sufficient progress in any one direction. (*Okay I've been on this keto plan for three days. Maybe I should try Intermittent Fasting instead.*)

The Distractor keeps us very, very busy — our lives are interesting and full — yet we don't seem to be getting anything done, we don't feel particularly fulfilled, and we always seem to be running late.

Our friends, families, and colleagues get fatigued trying to stay abreast of whatever's captured our fancy today. They get irritated at our constantly shifting priorities (*Hang on. I thought you were doing keto but now you want to do Intermittent Fasting?*)

The Overcomplicator

This internal rascal creates great drama out of simple situations. It can generate a thousand "what if's" and complications for any scenario...none of which are very likely or relevant. It can devise convoluted rationalizations to talk you into — or out of — absolutely anything.

This whirlwind of our over-active, over-thinking minds can be bewildering, intimidating, or annoying to those around us. We can introduce new information or options at a time when it doesn't seem relevant to the task at hand. We can share too many ideas at once, making others confused or uncomfortable. We can inadvertently squash other people's input.

Without meaning to, The Overcomplicator can push people away. They may not want to disturb us or challenge us in the midst of a brainstorm. We can give off a negative vibe. The volume of ideas we generate can be intimidating.

If you find yourself formulating a customized food plan that is, say, part Mediterranean, part paleo, part vegan, part Weight Watchers, and part South Beach, you are probably operating at the mercy of The Overcomplicator within.

The Quitter

When you hit a roadblock, The Quitter's knee-jerk response is to wail in despair, "We're doomed! We're done! We can't go on!"

The Quitter gives up at the slightest sign of difficulty. We end up walking away from perfectly viable plans . . . or delaying our progress unduly.

The Quitter may make our lives easier in the short term (*Okay, I tried that for a week. It didn't work*). However, this dooms us to dissatisfaction and unhappiness in the long term (*Nothing I do comes to anything.*)

The Quitter interferes with our efforts on things we actually yearn to do. When we don't do them, we feel guilty. We are plagued by regrets and disappointments and "if only's." We feel like failures. We can emit a "loser" energy that is off-putting to others.

When it comes to food plans, The Quitter stops us before we see the long-term results we are seeking.

ACTIVITY:

Re-read the descriptions of the Inner Saboteur. For each, rate to what extent each Inner Saboteur affects you. Use a scale of 1 - 10 in which "1" means "not at all" and "10" means "a lot." Highlight anything that seems particularly true for you.

Use your *Food Thoughts Journal* to write about each of your typical Inner Saboteurs.

- Under what circumstances has this Inner Saboteur surfaced?
- What did they cause you to do? What did you experience?
- What thoughts did they provoke? (Did this remind you of anything or anyone in your past?)

Everyone faces these inner enemies at some point in life.

YOU, however, have the advantage of understanding what's going on. You can recognize these inner forces when they arise. You take action to combat them.

➢ **Detect your Inner Saboteur**

Given the sneaky nature of these inner saboteurs, the trick is to detect them. *(Hmm. Why haven't I eaten mindfully for a month? Good grief! The Delayer strikes again!)*

Going forward, be vigilant. Keep an eye out for your most persistent Inner Saboteur.

Be attentive to what you are experiencing. If something feels unnecessarily fraught or stressful or complicated, pause and take stock. What are you thinking? What are you feeling? Ask yourself, "Is this my Inner Saboteur?"

Do you detect a little negative voice in your head? What is it saying?

Sometimes the easiest way to detect our Inner Saboteur is to watch for cues from others. How are the people around you responding to your words and actions? Which Inner Saboteur might be eliciting these reactions?

> **Take stock**

Process what is happening. Be specific.

What messages is the saboteur broadcasting in your brain?

What actions are you taking because of it? What actions are you avoiding?

How is this Inner Saboteur affecting the people around you?

The more specific you can be, the more opportunities you will have to combat your Inner Saboteur effectively.

> **Understand your Inner Saboteur**

Going forward, whenever you notice signs of your Inner Saboteur, understand that it's really trying to be your friend.

There's no need to be cross or frustrated with your Inner Saboteur. Instead, be thankful. Remember that your Inner Saboteur is actually your brain. It has detected a change and is trying to protect you from unknown dangers.

Once you understand this, you can respond differently. You don't have to take any resistance personally. It's not a reflection on your character, competence, or willpower. You are experiencing what happens to every person embarking on real personal change. Simply acknowledge what's happening and carry on in your desired direction.

When you recognize your Inner Saboteurs, you can counter them as they arise. When you get adept at this, you may even laugh at them. *(Hang on, why am I looking up Blue Zones recipes? Oh, there's ol' Distractor tempting me with another bright, shiny option. Nice try, D, but I'm going to stick with keto for this month at least.)*

Also realize that you must be getting some benefit out of this resistance — or you wouldn't be doing it. Maybe it's easier. Perhaps you're letting yourself off the hook. Maybe you're soothing yourself. Perhaps you're overwhelmed and, inside, are seeking a break from your plans. There is nothing inherently bad or wrong about these short-term benefits. Just make note of them. Whatever they are, they will give you clues about what are you experiencing deep down, what your real needs are, and how to move forward more effectively.

> **Take action**

The best remedy for any of these Inner Saboteurs is purposeful, directed action.

No matter which Inner Saboteur is at work, ask, "What is the simplest, easiest thing I could do to move forward with my plans?" This deceptively simple question is designed to disrupt every Inner Saboteur.

The Fear Monger dissipates with action. And action feels so much better than fear. Think of a time you were nervous to do something (speak in public, for example) but as soon as you began, your butterflies vanished. What a relief!

Similarly, The Delayer dissolves as soon as you start doing something. (Anything!)

The Judge is pretty good about moving forward. HOWEVER, you first need to suspend judgment about what you're doing. Understand that you can't accurately assess the quality of something while you're in the thick of it. Suspend judgment and keep going. If you hear negative inner messages (*This is not good enough!*), refute them (*I am aiming for progress, not perfection. I don't need to be executing my plans flawlessly. I just need to be moving in the desired direction.*)

Action prompts The Distractor to channel your efforts in one specific direction. Keep your focus on the action you have chosen. If a disrupting thought occurs to you, jot it down in your *Food Thoughts Journal*. It is captured and you can process it later if you *really* need to. But not right now. There is no reason to drop what you're doing and race off in a random direction.

The Overcomplicator is curtailed by the liberal use of the word "easy." Use this word as your magic wand. What's the *easiest* way to proceed? Do that. Then keep asking the question. What's the next easiest thing I can do? Go forward in the easiest way possible. If you are ever in doubt, choose what's easy.

If you're tempted by The Quitter, the action you can take is to ask, "Is it *really* quitting time or is there something easy I could do to continue forward with my plans?"

Bookmark the activity that follows. When you sense that you are resisting change, or that your Inner Saboteur is interfering with your desired plans, use these prompts to get back on track:

ACTIVITY: COUNTERING RESISTANCE TO CHANGE

Use your *Food Thoughts Journal* to answer the following:

1. What are you experiencing? What signs of resistance are you aware of?

   - What are you feeling? *(E.g., fear, dismay, disappointment.)*
   - What messages are you hearing? What is your Inner Saboteur saying to you?
   - What thoughts is it generating? *(If in doubt, scan your mind for any negative, painful statements about yourself or what you are doing.)*
   - What actions are you taking because of this Inner Saboteur?
   - What actions are you avoiding because of it?
   - What impact is this resistance having on the people around you?

2. Is a particular Inner Saboteur is causing you the most disruption at the moment? If so, name it.

3. What is your Inner Saboteur trying to protect you from? What are the benefits of the resistance you are experiencing?

4. Given your answers, do your plans require any adjustments?

5. What actions can you take to move forward? (The simpler, the easier, the better.)

ℋ

The purpose of this chapter has been to alert you to your natural resistance to change and to give you ways to counter any self-sabotage that arises. However, sometimes external obstacles arise that interfere with our plans. The next chapter is intended to help you overcome these possible setbacks.

Chapter 9

Overcome Setbacks

As you take steps to implement your preferred plans, it is likely that you will encounter obstacles along the way. Everyone experiences challenges. What differs is how different people deal with the hindrances they encounter. Some take it in stride and calmly move into problem-solving mode. Other people get thrown off track or paralyzed. They find themselves not doing what they really want to do. They feel awful. If that sounds familiar, this chapter is for you. As part of your planning process, you had the opportunity to inoculate yourself against some potential obstacles (page 64). By identifying likely challenges and generating potential solutions for each, you can be better prepared to deal with these setbacks, should they arise.

That sounds great in theory, but the truth is that when real obstacles occur, we tend to forget the obvious steps forward. I'm spelling them out here so you have a handy reminder:

1. Expect the unexpected

Going forward, know that unforeseen challenges and obstacles are likely to arise. When they do, acknowledge them, and move swiftly to find a way forward.

The sooner you can move from reaction *(Oh no! This rotten thing has happened! This is so unfair! My plans are doomed!)* to action (*Okay, what can I do about this?*), the less likely you are to stall or get thrown off track.

2. Generate possible solutions

When something goes awry, there's a natural tendency to pounce on the first solution you think of. That's good in that it moves you forward . . . but you may be missing out on a better alternative.

If possible, when you encounter an obstacle or challenge, pause to brainstorm a number of ideas to overcome it. To the extent you consider different options, you are more likely to choose a sounder way forward.

The key here is to be brief. Set a time limit (say, five minutes) and generate as many ideas as you can. Be sure to generate some far-fetched options, for example:

- How would my grandparent solve this?
- How would a scientist solve this?
- What would a five-year-old do?
- How would my personal hero respond?

Consider asking people you trust to help you brainstorm possible solutions to your challenge. When two or more minds are devoted to solving the same problem, you will be capitalizing on the wisdom, perspectives, and experiences of others. Your ideas can ping off each other into new and unforeseen solutions. You will devise a better way forward in a briefer period of time.

3. Evaluate your options

Review your options. Highlight what seems most promising.

If something seems far-fetched, ask, "Is there a kernel of an idea here that might work?" (*No, I can't "stop eating altogether." That's ridiculous. But what's a more practical option? Maybe I could designate certain times of the day as "non-eating" periods. Maybe I could try Intermittent Fasting. Maybe I could set a food curfew at night.*)

4. Select a solution

Assess your possible solutions. If there isn't an obvious, single, best way forward, use a point system to rate the possible solutions you have generated.

Choose among the options. What makes the most sense for you, given your current circumstances?

If in doubt, pick something. Pick anything. It really doesn't matter what you choose. Selecting ANY solution to move forward is better than staying stuck in your present circumstances.

5. Implement your solution

Take action. The sooner the better. If in doubt, pick the easiest, smallest step you can take to begin to implement your chosen solution. A journey of a thousand miles begins with a single step. Every act moving forward in your desired direction is an accomplishment.

6. Monitor your progress and adjust as needed

From time to time, check in to assess how things are going. If your solution is working well, great. Carry on. Make note of any lessons learned. Reward yourself for finding an effective solution.

If you need to adjust your plans, do so.

If you need to try something else entirely, review your list of options and choose a different solution to implement.

Ж

Common Setbacks and Their Solutions

No matter how well we plan, regardless of all the precautions we take to stay on track, sometimes when we set out to make real, personal change, we encounter obstacles that affect our progress. Here are four common ones — and their solutions.

Setback #1: Life Intervenes

It is astonishing how often life intervenes when people embark on a particular course of action. They have made a commitment to change, they are eager to implement their plans, and blam! they are broadsided by an unexpected turn of events.

John just started his new food plan and suddenly received three dinner party invitations. Kari began her meditation practice and within weeks, her relatives descended on her, disrupting her newfound mindful calm. Andrea pre-paid for a year at the gym and before she could go once, she fractured her fibula.

Another common occurrence when someone is embarking on real change is a plague of minor irritations. For example, while Maria was making real strides in managing her food cravings, she experienced a flurry of random technical troubles. Her phone went on the fritz, dropping calls like never before. Emails that she thought she had sent weren't transmitted. Her alarm clock failed to go off, the morning of an important meeting. Her dishwasher stopped functioning.

"Excellent," I told her. "These are 'Change Gremlins' and they signal that you are making real progress. Laugh at them when you notice them, deal with them, and carry on."

Sometimes challenges arise in several areas of life in quick succession. For example, just after Anna committed to overcoming her nighttime snacking, she suddenly faced a tsunami of challenges. Her mother got cancer. Her husband asked for a divorce. Her daughter dropped out of college. She w

as forced to sell her house. She had to find a new job. That's a lot of challenges! It was a difficult period but Anna did get through it and was then able to resume her plans with a new wisdom and broader perspective she could apply to her efforts.

How to get back on track:

> **Make good self-care your top priority**

Be kind and compassionate with yourself (Chapter 7). If you don't take care of yourself first, you can't take care of anyone else who depends on you, nor can you deal with any of your priorities.

> **Accept what you can't change; change what you can**

Understand that sometimes, unfortunately, bad things happen to good people. Bad things happen to everyone at some point, actually, so this is just part of life. You can't change the event but you can change your reaction to it.

> **Know that, whatever it is, you'll handle it**

It may be unpleasant. It may be difficult. But you *will* get through this, just as you've gotten through everything else you've experienced thus far in life.

> **Adjust your time line**

It's okay to tweak your plans. Focus on progress, rather than perfection. If you have to pause your plans, do so purposefully. Return to them when possible. When it makes sense — when you believe that you're through the bulk of whatever you're dealing with — re-assess your priorities, then amend your plans accordingly.

Setback # 2: Others Interfere

Sometimes, people may interfere with your plans for random reasons. Sometimes, somebody might intend to support you … but may say or do things that obstruct your progress.

If someone responds to your efforts with something like, "Why go to all that trouble? You don't really expect to change at your age, do you?"— that's pretty overt, direct opposition to your plans. It's pretty easy to recognize and handle.

However, most interference is more subtle. Sometimes a lukewarm response to your plans is all that's needed to dampen your enthusiasm. Let's say you're all fired up about your new food program and when you tell someone about it, they say, "Meh" and change the subject. That can quash your motivation and make you question the value of something that you've chosen as a priority.

Be vigilant about the affect others have on you and your plans. Protect yourself from undue, unhelpful influences.

Recognize that others' interference can be intentional or subconscious.

Let's say you're doing your darndest to avoid snacking and your partner keeps offering you ice cream or comes home with armloads of your favorite junk food. Now your partner *may* be aware that these actions aren't helpful, but not necessarily. It could be that, subconsciously, your partner doesn't want you to change because of a fear of losing you. Or maybe they don't want to feel pressured to change their own eating habits. Perhaps, deep down, they are jealous of the progress you are making. Or maybe they just want you to be happy and you've been pretty cranky lately, as you fight your food cravings.

One thing to keep in mind is that the reactions of others may have little to do with you and much more to do with their own issues and challenges. When you recognize that someone is interfering with your plans, consider why that might be.

> **ACTIVITY:**
> Think of a time in which someone interfered with what you were trying to do, dampened your enthusiasm, or hampered your progress.
> 1. What did the person say or do?
> 2. How did you react?
> 3. What were the short-term and longer-term consequences?
> 4. How did you get back on track?
> 5. If you encounter a similar situation in the future, how would you like to handle it?

How to get back on track:

How you deal with interference by others will depend on the situation, the person, and your relationship to them. Use your good judgment.

If it's someone important to you, of course you'll talk about it. You might say something like, "When you say or do [_____], the impact on me is [_____]. I'd rather you say or do [_____] because that would be more helpful." *(When you buy junk food, it's frustrating for me. I'm trying to avoid snacking and having temptations in the house makes it more difficult. It'd help me if you would either avoid buying junk food or if you would keep it out of the house — like in your car or at your workplace.)*

If it's someone you don't trust, or someone who means little to you, you're probably better off saying nothing to them. Instead, remind yourself that they have no effect on you unless you let them.

Regardless of who has interfered:

> ➤ **Remind yourself of your true motivation (page 60) for what you are undertaking**

What is the Big Picture here? What are you trying to achieve? Why?

> ➤ **Rely on the support you have chosen (page 62)**

If your chosen support person is the one sabotaging your efforts, shield yourself from them and find a new source of support.

> **Be vigilant about monitoring your progress (page 65)**

Make adjustments as needed.

Setback # 3: You Get Stuck, Stalled, or Derailed

Sometimes it can feel like you have plateaued. It might be that you discover you're on the wrong path. Or you might find yourself blocked, paused, or at a dead stop.

Whenever you recognize you're not making progress, pat yourself on the back. You noticed! Now you can do something about it.

How to get back on track:

> **Be kind to yourself**

Avoid berating yourself for the situation. It doesn't help to be disappointed with yourself or to call yourself negative names. You are a smart, competent person with a lot going on. Give yourself some credit. Treat yourself as you would treat a friend in the same situation.

Know that we *all* have "those" days sometimes. *Everyone* gets stuck or finds themselves off course at some point. It's human nature. *No one* is operating at their ideal capacity, every hour of every day, every day of the week, every week of the year, every year of their lives.

> **Assess the situation**

Once you realize you're stalled, ask yourself, "Why?"

Is it fear? Are you anxious about how things are unfolding? Are you concerned about something?

Is it fatigue? Do you need a mental or physical break?

Are you excessively stressed?

Is it that you are not seeing results and/or you've hit some vexing obstacle?

Is it that you are facing other challenges in life that are affecting your plans? Is your life unbalanced?

Perhaps a combination of factors is at play. What's your best guess about what's going on? If you're not sure, write about it in your *Food Thoughts Journal* (page 4). Putting pen to paper to describe the situation has a way of unlocking the truth.

➢ Put things in context

This is where your *Food Thoughts Journal* can be invaluable. Review what you've written. How does your current situation fit into the Big Picture — your history, your plans, your experiences so far?

What progress have you made?

What do you know about yourself? What can apply to your current situation?

➢ Devise a course of action

Once you determine what's going on, you can do what makes sense: Face your fears, take a break, brainstorm solutions. What do you need to do to address whatever has caused you to become stuck, stalled, or derailed?

If in doubt, ask, "What's the simplest, easiest thing I could do to move forward?"

Many of us tend to feel like "it doesn't count" if we're not tackling complicated things. Doing anything less challenging can feel like "cheating" or "laziness." Doing "less" or doing something "easy" feels wrong. This is a false belief that makes it difficult to get back on track.

Doing something easy is not wrong. In fact, it's completely necessary. If you're stuck, stalled, or derailed, allowing yourself to do something easy is actually the only effective way forward.

➢ Remind yourself why you're doing this in the first place

Review your notes in your *Food Thoughts Journal*: What was your original motivation? Does that still apply? (If not, why are you beating yourself up, trying to do it? Do something else.) If yes, what benefits are there to doing what you're doing? Literally write down as many reasons as you can. Rekindle your original passion.

➢ Choose to press the "reset button"

Make a conscious decision to move forward. You can't do anything about what has happened. You can't change the amount of time you've been stalled. But you *can* decide to change course going forward.

You have the right to a fresh start. Right now.

It doesn't matter what time of day it is. It doesn't matter what day of the week it is. It doesn't matter how long you've been stalled. Right now, in this very moment, you can decide to change course.

You have power over this particular moment in time. You can choose to get unstuck, to get back on track, and to move forward.

Press the "reset button." Take action.

Your initial goal should be simply to **start (page 68)**. Something. Anything. Just start. Feel good about it. Avoid judging the size or significance of what you've done. Focus on any forward motion.

➢ **Reward yourself for resuming (page 28 and 67)**

Once you start to move forward, be very, very proud of yourself. Any forward motion is to be appreciated and rewarded. Monitor your progress and give yourself some treats to acknowledge your accomplishment and to reinforce your forward momentum.

➢ **Aim for gradual improvements**

As you get going, continue to focus on any movement in your desired direction. Aim for progress, not perfections. Document every win. Build your momentum. In all likelihood, once you get restarted, you'll accelerate your progress faster than you expect.

Ж

Moving Forward

I hope you've found the techniques and activities in this book helpful in overcoming your emotional eating. Your stories, feedback and suggestions for improvement on this book are most welcome. Please contact me here: **http://bit.ly/contactliisakyle**

Many of my readers find they'd like more support and personalized help in making desired changes in their lives, overcoming challenges, and achieving their goals.

I offer **three-month coaching packages** tailored to accomplish your specific objectives, no matter where you are in the world. Working with me, using a dynamic combination of live one-on-one phone, Zoom, or Skype sessions, personalized fieldwork activities, and email support, in just 90 days you can:

- ✓ figure out what you really want — and what you really don't
- ✓ achieve your goals faster, easier, and with less stress
- ✓ identify and overcome whatever has been holding you back or interfering with your success
- ✓ overcome obstacles you encounter more effectively, more efficiently, and more easily
- ✓ do more of what you love and less of what you don't
- ✓ manage your time more effectively and efficiently
- ✓ gain a deeper understanding of your core strengths and learn how to make the most of them
- ✓ acquire a better understanding of different areas of your life and how to make real improvements in them
- ✓ achieve an improved work/life balance
- ✓ improve your personal and professional relationships
- ✓ enjoy your life more

I've helped people make real, significant changes in their life — and I'd love to do the same for you. Tell me how I can help. Simply fill out this short online form to let me know what you'd like to get out of coaching, your preferred contact information, and any relevant info you'd care to share: **http://bit.ly/contactliisakyle**

Note: Your information is 100% confidential and filling out the form doesn't commit you to anything.

If you'd like to receive free weekly email prompts to foster your personal development, please sign up here: **http://bit.ly/weeklyprompts**

Wishing you all the best,

Liisa Kyle, Ph.D.

About the Author

Liisa Kyle, Ph.D. is the go-to coach for smart, creative people who want to overcome challenges, get things done, and get more out of life. For the past twenty years, she has coached individuals, facilitated groups, and delivered inventive workshops on four continents (www.LiisaKyle.com, www.CoachingForCreativePeople.com).

She earned her Ph.D. in Psychology from the University of Michigan and has authored two dozen books about topics including:

- happiness
- creativity
- getting things done
- goal-setting and planning
- self-worth
- overcoming procrastination
- overcoming perfectionism
- overcoming emotional eating
- getting over regrets, disappointments and past mistakes
- how to make the most of your retirement
- how to make the most of a milestone birthday, and
- how to make real, directed, personal change

Liisa Kyle co-founded The DaVinci Dilemma™ — an online community devoted to helping smart, creative people juggling too many talents, too many projects, and too many ideas. Check out her free self-help articles at www.DavinciDilemma.com.

To arrange personal one-on-one coaching, corporate consultation, workshops, or public speaking appearances:
bit.ly/contactliisakyle

For Free Weekly E-Mail Self-Coaching Prompts:
bit.ly/weeklyprompts

Coaching Special Offers: bit.ly/LKspecialoffer

Acknowledgements:

Heartfelt thanks to everyone who shared their food stories with me. Your candor and generosity in sharing such personal information is much appreciated.

Sincere thanks to Lori Atkinson, Glenna Quinn Felsman, Lisa Kraus, Cheryl Lyte, and Janna Stewart for reading earlier drafts of this book.

In gratitude for many blessings, a portion of this proceeds of this book is being donated to charity.

YOU CAN CHANGE YOUR LIFE
A Workbook to Become the Person You Want to Be

Liisa Kyle, Ph.D.

Self-Worth Essentials
A Workbook to Understand Yourself, Accept Yourself, Like Yourself, Respect Yourself, Be Confident, Enjoy Yourself, and Love Yourself

Liisa Kyle, Ph.D.

You Can Get It Done
CHOOSE WHAT TO DO,
PLAN,
START,
STAY ON TRACK,
OVERCOME OBSTACLES,
AND FINISH

Liisa Kyle, Ph.D.

Making the Most of Your Retirement
WAYS TO FOSTER HEALTH, HAPPINESS & FULFILLMENT AT ANY AGE

Liisa Kyle, Ph.D.

MAKING THE MOST OF 2024
A WORKBOOK

Liisa Kyle, Ph.D.

COPING IN TIMES OF CRISIS
WAYS TO HANDLE UNCERTAINTY AND NAVIGATE THE UNKNOWN FUTURE

Liisa Kyle, Ph.D.

KNOW YOURSELF BETTER
Self-Discovery Questions and Activities

Liisa Kyle, Ph.D.

Be More Creative
101 ACTIVITIES TO UNLEASH AND GROW YOUR CREATIVITY

Liisa Kyle, Ph.D.

COACH YOURSELF
SELF-COACHING QUESTIONS & ACTIVITIES FOR SELF-DISCOVERY AND PERSONAL GROWTH

LIISA KYLE, PH.D.

40 WAYS to ENJOY TURNING FORTY
Make the Most of your Milestone Birthday to Have the Best Year Ever

Liisa Kyle, Ph.D.

50 WAYS to ENJOY TURNING FIFTY
Make the Most of Your Milestone Birthday to Have the Best Year Ever

Liisa Kyle, Ph.D.

Making the Most of Your MILESTONE BIRTHDAY
52 Ways to Have the Best Year Ever

Liisa Kyle, Ph.D.

Life Levers
MAKE SMALL CHANGES TO CREATE BIG IMPROVEMENTS IN YOUR LIFE

Liisa Kyle, Ph.D.

Get Over It
Overcome Regret, Disappointment and Past Mistakes

Liisa Kyle, Ph.D.

Overcoming Perfectionism
Solutions for Perfectionists

Liisa Kyle, Ph.D.

OVERCOME EMOTIONAL EATING
Coach Yourself to Manage Cravings, Eat Mindfully, and Foster a Healthy Relationship with Food

LIISA KYLE, Ph.D.

ACCEPTANCE: A Workshop for Perfectionists
Overcome perfectionism by learning to accept circumstances, accept others as they are and self-acceptance

By Liisa Kyle, Ph.D.

Coping with the Virus Crisis
WAYS TO HANDLE UNCERTAINTY AND NAVIGATE THE NEW NORMAL

Liisa Kyle, Ph.D.

Manufactured by Amazon.ca
Bolton, ON